P9-CFM-775

How to Use This Book

Look for these special features in this book:

SIDEBARS, **CHARTS**, **GRAPHS**, and original **MAPS** expand your understanding of what's being discussed—and also make useful sources for classroom reports.

FAQs answer common **F**requently **A**sked **Q**uestions about people, places, and things.

WOW FACTORS offer "Who knew?" facts to keep you thinking.

TRAVEL GUIDE gives you tips on exploring the state—either in person or right from your chair!

PROJECT ROOM provides fun ideas for school assignments and incredible research projects. Plus, there's a guide to primary sources—what they are and how to cite them.

Please note: All statistics are as up-to-date as possible at the time of publication.

Consultants: Jon Axline, Historian, Montana Department of Transportation; Richard I. Gibson, Consulting Geologist, Butte, Montana; William Loren Katz

Book production by The Design Lab

Library of Congress Cataloging-in-Publication Data
Stein, R. Conrad.
 Montana / by R. Conrad Stein.
    p. cm.—(America the beautiful, third series)
 Includes bibliographical references and index.
 ISBN-13: 978-0-531-18500-1
 ISBN-10: 0-531-18500-1
 1. Montana—Juvenile literature. I. Title. II. Series.
 F731.3.S74 2009
 978.6—dc22   2008000823

1 2 3 4 5 6 7 8 9 10 R 19 18 17 16 15 14 13 12 11 10

AMERICA ★ THE ★ BEAUTIFUL

Montana

BY R. CONRAD STEIN

Third Series

Children's Press®
An Imprint of Scholastic Inc.
New York ★ Toronto ★ London ★ Auckland ★ Sydney
Mexico City ★ New Delhi ★ Hong Kong
Danbury, Connecticut

CONTENTS

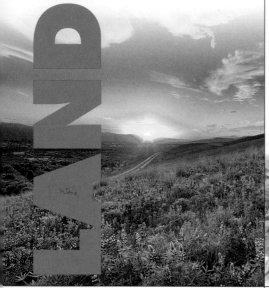

GROWTH AND CHANGE

4

Mining towns go boom and bust, Native Americans fight to keep their lands, and railroads bring thousands of settlers to the region. **42**

MORE MODERN TIMES

5

Copper becomes king, women win the right to vote, and people across the country begin to appreciate Montana's magnificent scenery. **58**

9 TRAVEL GUIDE

From craggy mountains to historic forts to ghost towns, there's plenty to keep you busy in Montana. . . . **106**

CANADA

N W E S

Kootenai
National Forest

Glacier National Park

Milk

Lewis and Clark
National Historic Trail
Interpretive Center

Louis Toavs John Deere
Tractor Collection and Museum

KALISPELL ○

Rocky

Montana
Historical Society

National
Bison Range

Flathead
Lake

Clark

Fork

MISSOULA ○

HELENA ★

Missouri

MONTANA

Fort
Peck
Lake

Western
Heritage Center

Mountains

Musselshell

Yellowstone

MILES CITY

Elkhorn
Ghost Town

◆ BUTTE ○

BOZEMAN ○

Granite Peak

BILLINGS

Bighorn

Custer
National Forest

The World
Museum of Mining

Yellowstone National
Park Gateways

Little Bighorn Battlefield
National Monument

IDAHO

WYOMING

0   50
Miles

Welcome to Montana!

HOW DID MONTANA GET ITS NAME?

In 1863, the area that would become Montana was preparing to become a political unit called a territory, which was the first step toward applying for statehood. Rugged mountains stretch across much of the region, and James Ashley, a U.S. congressman, proposed that the territory be called Montana, which is Spanish for "mountainous." The following year, when Montana became a territory, that became its official name.

MONTANA

8

READ
ABOUT

A view of
Swiftcurrent
Lake and Mount
Wilbur in Glacier
National Park

CHAPTER ONE

LAND

★

MONTANA IS HUGE. It stretches across 147,042 square miles (380,837 square kilometers), making it the nation's fourth-largest state. Mountains rise in the western portion of the state, and gently rolling plains cover eastern Montana. The state has several nicknames. One is the Land of Shining Mountains, because of its many snowcapped peaks. The state's highest point, Granite Peak, rises 12,799 feet (3,901 meters) above sea level. Even Montana's lowest point at the Kootenai River is 1,800 feet (549 m) high.

Researchers work to uncover dinosaur fossils at a site near Roundup.

SEE IT HERE!

MUSEUM OF THE ROCKIES

Dinosaurs, including the fearsome *Tyrannosaurus rex*, once roamed in Montana. The Museum of the Rockies in Bozeman displays dinosaur bones uncovered in Montana fossil beds. The museum has exhibits of dinosaur nests and shows the bones of many species not found elsewhere. Besides learning about dinosaurs, museum visitors can also find out about the people and history of Montana.

GEOLOGICAL PAST

More than 300 million years ago, a warm, shallow sea covered most of what is now Montana. Several times over millions of years, the seas in Montana retreated and then returned. Between 65 million and 200 million years ago, Montana was covered by rich plant life. During this time, many dinosaurs roamed the Montana region. Today, Montana is one of the best places in the world to find dinosaur fossils.

Some 60 million to 80 million years ago, great upheavals in the earth's surface raised the western part of the state.

THE STATE FOSSIL

Montana is one of the world's richest sources of dinosaur fossils. In 1985, the government chose the duck-billed dinosaur as the official state fossil. The scientific name for the duck-billed dinosaur is *Maiasaura peeblesorum*, meaning "good mother lizard." Evidence suggests they were good mothers. At Egg Mountain (named for the many dinosaur eggs found there) near Choteau, scientists discovered nests that duck-billed dinosaurs made some 135 million years ago. The nests, which measured 6 feet (1.8 m) in diameter, held eggs that mother duckbills tended. Dinosaur skeletons uncovered at Egg Mountain indicate that baby duckbills were about the size of today's house cats, and adults were 30 feet (9 m) long.

Later, violent volcanic activity helped form the Rocky Mountains in this region.

JACK HORNER: PALEONTOLOGIST

Jack Horner (1946–), who was born in Shelby, developed a consuming interest in dinosaurs as a child. He was fortunate to have been born in Montana, which is rich in fossils, and he discovered his first dinosaur fossil at age six. He became a paleontologist, a person who studies early animal and plant life. He now heads the paleontology department at the Museum of the Rockies in Bozeman. Horner is the author of *Dinosaurs Under the Big Sky*, a book about the great animals that once lived in his home state, known as Big Sky Country. He also served as an adviser for the Jurassic Park movies, which are about scientists who bring dinosaurs to life.

 Want to know more? See www.museumofthe rockies.org/Home/EXPLORE/Dinosaurs/Paleo Department/JackHorner/tabid/389/Default.aspx

LAND REGIONS

On a map, Montana looks like a rectangle with a bite taken out of its lower left-hand corner. The line of the bite is formed by the Bitterroot Range, which is part of the Rocky Mountains. The Bitterroot Range serves as the boundary between Montana and Idaho, which lies to the west. To the north, Montana has a long border with Canada. To the east, the state borders North and South Dakota. Wyoming lies to the south.

WOW

A drive along Montana's entire northern border is about 550 miles (885 km), or roughly equal to a drive between New York City and Chicago, Illinois.

A hiker in the Beartooth Mountains

Montana Geo-Facts

Along with the state's geographical highlights, this chart ranks Montana's land, water, and total area compared to all other states.

Total area; rank . . . . . 147,042 square miles (380,837 sq km); 4th
Land; rank . . . . 145,552 square miles (376,978 sq km); 4th
Water; rank . . . . 1,490 square miles (3,859 sq km); 26th
Inland water; rank . . . . . . 1,490 square miles (3,859 sq km); 15th
Geographic center . Fergus County, 11 miles (18 km) west of Lewistown
Latitude . . . . .44°26' N to 49° N
Longitude . . . . 104°2' W to 116°2' W
Highest point . . . . .Granite Peak, 12,799 feet (3,901 m),
in Park County
Lowest point . . . Kootenai River in Lincoln County, 1,800 feet (549 m)
Largest city . . . . Billings
Longest river . . . . Missouri

Source: U.S. Census Bureau

Rhode Island, the smallest state, could fit inside Montana 95 times!

Montana falls into two North American land regions: the Great Plains and the Rocky Mountains.

The Great Plains

The eastern two-thirds of Montana lies in the Great Plains, a region extending from Canada to Mexico. In Montana, the Great Plains is made up of flatlands, rolling hills, and small mountain chains.

Montana Topography

Use the color-coded elevation chart to see on the map Montana's high points (dark red to orange) and low points (green to dark green). Elevation is measured as the distance above or below sea level.

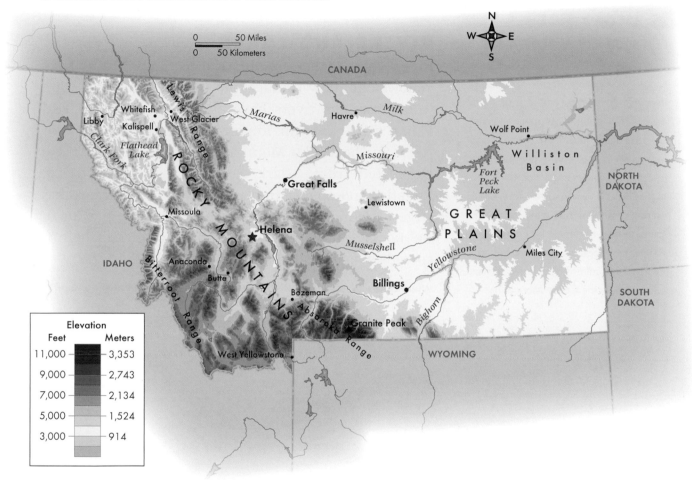

Elevation	
Feet	Meters
11,000	3,353
9,000	2,743
7,000	2,134
5,000	1,524
3,000	914

The Rocky Mountains

The rugged Rocky Mountains run about 3,000 miles (4,828 km) from northern New Mexico to Alaska. They cover about the western one-third of Montana. Individual mountain ranges within Montana's Rockies include the Beartooth, Big Belt, Bitterroot, Cabinet,

Some of the oldest rocks in North America are in the Beartooth Mountains. They are almost 3 billion years old.

SEE IT HERE!

THE CRAZY MOUNTAINS

The Crazy Mountains make up a wild range containing many confusing intersecting valleys. Hundreds of years ago, Crow people escaped enemies by retreating into the Crazies and hiding in its maze-like valleys. Some people say the range got its name in the 1800s when a woman on a wagon train lost her mind and was found talking to herself in the foothills. At first, the range was called the Crazy Woman Mountains, but later it was called simply the Crazy Mountains.

Crazy, Flathead, Little Belt, Absaroka, Lewis, Mission, and Swan. Their peaks are snowcapped eight to ten months a year. Some are so rough and jagged that they have never been climbed.

RIVERS AND LAKES

Rivers such as the Missouri and its major branch, the Yellowstone, flow through the Great Plains. Irrigation water from the rivers have allowed Montana's Great Plains to become an important farming area. Major rivers in the Rocky Mountain region include the Big Hole, Bitterroot, Clark Fork, Blackfoot, Flathead, Gallatin, Kootenai, Jefferson, and Madison. The state's largest natural lake is Flathead Lake, which nestles in the Rocky Mountains south of the city of Kalispell. It spreads over 188 square miles (487 sq km).

Wild Horse Island, located in Flathead Lake, is accessible only by boat.

The Continental Divide runs through Montana in the Rocky Mountains. Montana is unique because it is the only state from which water drains in three directions. The Missouri River and its **tributaries** eventually empty into the Gulf of Mexico. Waters in the Clark Fork run into the Columbia River system and then to the Pacific Ocean. The St. Mary and its sister rivers begin in the northern Rocky Mountains, flow into Canada, and eventually reach the Atlantic Ocean at Hudson Bay.

CLIMATE

Montana is divided into two climate zones. The Rocky Mountain region tends to be wetter and warmer than the Great Plains to the east. The state averages 11 inches (28 centimeters) of rain and about 15 inches (38 cm) of snow per year. But Montana is large and varied. Parts of the Rocky Mountains, for example, receive more than 300 inches (762 cm) of snowfall in a typical winter season. May and June are the wettest months for most of the state.

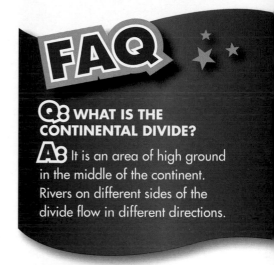

Q8 WHAT IS THE CONTINENTAL DIVIDE?

A8 It is an area of high ground in the middle of the continent. Rivers on different sides of the divide flow in different directions.

WOW

On January 20, 1954, the temperature at Rogers Pass dropped to –70°F (–57°C). It was the coldest temperature ever recorded in the United States outside of Alaska.

Weather Report

This chart shows record temperatures (high and low) for the state, as well as average temperatures (July and January) and average annual precipitation.

Record high temperature . . . . 117°F (47°C) at Glendive on July 20, 1893, and at Medicine Lake on July 5, 1937
Record low temperature . . . . . . –70°F (–57°C) at Rogers Pass on January 20, 1954
Average July temperature .68°F (20°C)
Average January temperature . . . . 20°F (–7°C)
Average yearly precipitation . . . . .11 inches (28 cm)

Source: National Climatic Data Center, NESDIS, NOAA, U.S. Department of Commerce

A wildfire near Billings, in August 2007

Montanans are accustomed to extreme weather, but the summer of 2007 took everyone by surprise. It was the hottest, driest summer in memory. In August, lightning lit the parched land, starting a wildfire that scorched some 400,000 acres (162,000 hectares) of western Montana. Many families had to leave their homes in the town of Seeley Lake as the flames approached. Also in August, temperatures soared above 100°F (38°C) for days at a time at Missoula. It was so hot that trout began to die off because they cannot survive when river waters get too warm. Officials banned fishing between 2 P.M. and midnight to give the trout a better chance to survive.

PLANT LIFE

A vast sea of grass once covered the Great Plains. It stretched from horizon to horizon. The native grass was called buffalo grass because it supported huge herds of bison, which are also called buffalo. A cattleman who came to Montana in the 1800s stood on the grasslands and remarked, "You could graze all the cattle in the world upon this plain." This is exactly what he and his fellow ranchers tried to do. By the early 1900s, Montana's Great Plains was a patchwork of small farms and large cattle and sheep ranches. The native grasses largely disappeared because too many animals grazed on them.

Woodlands cover about one-fourth of the state, with nine national forests lying within Montana. Alder, birch, fir, pine, and spruce are common trees. More than 2,500 species of wildflowers and nonflowering plants can be found in the state. Typical flowers that bloom in Montana include aster, daisy, lily, poppy, and bitterroot, the state flower.

W⭐W

Montana has 19 million acres (7.7 million ha) of national forestland, an area roughly equal to the entire state of South Carolina.

Bitterroot, the state flower

A field of lupine wildflowers in the Bitterroot Range

The pronghorn is the fastest mammal in North America and the second fastest in the world. Only the cheetah can outrun it.

Many pronghorn live in the Rocky Mountain region.

ANIMAL LIFE

In 1805, Meriwether Lewis and William Clark led a group of explorers through what is now Montana. They were the first European Americans to enter the region. Walking alone one day in June, Lewis heard a roar that sounded like thunder. The earth below him shook. He climbed a hill and saw "infinitely more buffalo than I had ever before witnessed at a view." The herd covered the grasslands like a dark cloud. Lewis and Clark also saw deer, bears, and "vast herds" of antelope. Streams were so crowded with fish, Lewis reported, that "I caught upwards of a dozen in a few minutes."

Although Montana no longer has the incredible wealth of animals that astonished Lewis and Clark, it is still rich in wildlife. Deer and bears inhabit all parts of

ENDANGERED SPECIES

Although Montana is filled with rugged and remote land, some species in the state have lost habitat or been overhunted, making them **endangered**. Montana's list of endangered species includes the black-footed ferret, the least tern, the pallid sturgeon, the white sturgeon, and the whooping crane. **Threatened** animals that live in Montana include the bald eagle, the bull trout, the Canada lynx, the grizzly bear (the state animal), and the piping plover.

the state. Herds of bison live on the plains. Pronghorn, a type of antelope, lope about the Rocky Mountain region. In the mountains are elk, moose, and mountain goats. Beavers and muskrats paddle in streams. Ducks and geese soar through the sky, while wild turkeys and pheasants nest on the ground. Trout abound in Montana's rivers.

The whooping crane is an endangered species that is native to Montana.

WORDS TO KNOW

endangered *in danger of becoming extinct*

threatened *likely to become endangered in the foreseeable future*

SEE IT HERE!

NATIONAL BISON RANGE

With a little imagination, you can experience the thrill of the early explorers when they saw herds of bison sweeping over the plains of Montana. At the National Bison Range near Missoula, wild bison are protected and nurtured. The federal government established the National Bison Range in 1908, after the numbers of bison had dwindled so dramatically in the United States that they were in danger of disappearing entirely. Now 300 to 500 bison thrive in this 19,000-acre (7,700 ha) reserve. Deer, bighorn sheep, and elk also live there.

Montana National Park Areas

This map shows some of Montana's national parks, monuments, preserves, and other areas protected by the National Park Service.

Waterton Lakes NP
(Canada)

CANADA

Glacier
NP
West Glacier

Kalispell

Flathead
Lake

Clark Fork

Marias

Milk

Havre

Missouri

Wolf Point

Missouri

NORTH
DAKOTA

Lewis and
Clark NHT

Fort
Peck
Lake

Continental
Divide NST

Great Falls

Missouri

Musselshell

N
W · E
S

Lewis and
Clark NHT

Missoula

Grant-Kohrs
Ranch NHS

Helena

Lewistown

Nez Perce
(Nee-Me-Poo)
NHT

Yellowstone

Miles City

Anaconda

Butte

Billings

Bighorn

Little Bighorn
Battlefield NM

SOUTH
DAKOTA

IDAHO

Big Hole
NB

Bozeman

Bighorn Canyon NRA

West Yellowstone

WYOMING

Yellowstone NP

0   50 Miles
0   50 Kilometers

⬛ National Park area	
NB	National Battlefield
NHS	National Historic Site
NHT	National Historic Trail
NM	National Monument
NP	National Park
NRA	National Recreation Area
NST	National Scenic Trail

HUMANS AND THE ENVIRONMENT

Montana is filled with spectacular natural scenery. Most Montanans appreciate their state's beauty and want to preserve it, yet people have to make a living and get to and from their workplaces. Often the state must balance these two goals. The state government is usually the final judge as to whether a new highway

Montanans work to preserve the environment for everyone's enjoyment.

should be built through the mountains or whether a housing complex should go up near a forested lake.

Energy is required to produce the electricity used in homes and businesses. Montana has a plentiful source of energy in what is called coal bed methane (CBM), a natural gas that is found in coal beds. Water traps the gas in coal beds. By pumping the water from the coal-field, it is possible to extract the CBM. The problem is what to do with the water. Water from coal beds has a high salt content that makes it unsuitable for irrigating fields. Coal bed water also has high levels of ammonia, sulfates, and other chemicals, so dumping it into rivers would threaten fish and other wildlife.

It is up to the Montana government to create laws dealing with the wastewater from the coal beds. But average Montanans and state lawmakers must all work together to help their state prosper while preserving its magnificent scenery.

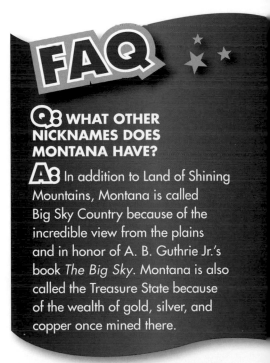

FAQ

Q8 WHAT OTHER NICKNAMES DOES MONTANA HAVE?

A8 In addition to Land of Shining Mountains, Montana is called Big Sky Country because of the incredible view from the plains and in honor of A. B. Guthrie Jr.'s book *The Big Sky*. Montana is also called the Treasure State because of the wealth of gold, silver, and copper once mined there.

READ ABOUT

Hunters from
Asia crossing the
Bering Strait some
15,000 years ago

c. 10,000 BCE

*People first arrive in
today's Montana*

c. 3000 BCE

*A drought grips the
Great Plains, driving
people and animals
from the region*

c. 1 CE ▲

*The drought ends, and
people (as well as bison)
return to Montana*

CHAPTER TWO

FIRST PEOPLE

★

GLACIERS ONCE COVERED MUCH OF NORTH AMERICA. Around 15,000 years ago, temperatures began to rise, ice melted, and the glaciers retreated. Some people from Asia made their way across the Bering Strait, a wide stretch of land that once connected Asia with today's Alaska. Others may have crossed in boats. Over time, the people spread throughout the Americas.

▲ c. 500
People in Montana begin using bows and arrows

1700s
Shoshones and other Native groups move into Montana

1800
Dozens of Native nations live in Montana

These Native Americans hunted bison by disguising themselves as wolves.

WORDS TO KNOW

archaeologists *people who study the remains of past human societies*

artifacts *items created by humans, usually for a practical purpose*

PEOPLE ARRIVE

Archaeologists believe that most people took what is called the Great North Trail in their journey to the south. The Great North Trail was a relatively ice-free path that stretched along the eastern slope of the Rocky Mountains. While trekking down this trail, the travelers found animals to hunt, wood for fires, and caves for shelter. **Artifacts** such as knives made from animal bones and stone spear points have been found along the Great North Trail, indicating that it was a major roadway for the earliest North Americans.

It is not known exactly when men and women entered what is now Montana. Many archaeologists estimate the first people arrived there around 12,000 years ago. Some experts believe Montana's original residents came thousands of years earlier.

Throughout Montana, archaeologists have discovered stone circles, called tipi rings, on the ground. The tipi rings could have been used to hold down the edges of tipis, small houses made from animal skins. Some people believe the rings had a religious function and served as altars.

The first Montanans hunted large animals such as mammoths and bison. The mammoths disappeared thousands of years ago, but the bison remained, continuing to provide food for people. A prolonged drought gripped the Great Plains 5,000 years ago, driving away people and animals. Some 2,000 years ago, the rains returned, grasses grew on the plains, the bison came back, and so did the people.

ANCIENT WAYS

Early Montanans sometimes used tools to help them hunt. One of their common hunting tools was the atlatl, a stick with a cup at one end. The hunter put the end of the spear into the cup and then used the stick to throw the spear. With the atlatl, the spear would go farther and with greater force, allowing the hunter to kill animals from a longer distance. About 500 CE, people in today's Montana began using the bow and arrow, which was more accurate than throwing a spear. Today, archaeologists search for arrowheads at the sites of ancient settlements. The arrowheads identify different stages of ancient people's development.

In the mountains, the ancient Montanans hunted deer and elk. They also fished in streams and gathered berries. They knew which plants could be used to cure illnesses. Early Montana mountain dwellers lived in communities of a dozen or more people. They moved frequently as they hunted.

The people of the plains relied mainly on bison for food. In the days before horses and guns, hunting

FORMED FROM CLAY

For centuries, Montana Native Americans have said that their ancestors were created in Montana and have always lived there. The Blackfoot people believe they were created along the Milk River in northern Montana. Their creator, Old Man, formed them out of clay and taught them to hunt bison. Old Man left the Blackfoot people and went west after he was satisfied that the people had learned hunting well enough to survive on their own. He vowed to return someday and bring with him vast herds of bison.

A spear thrown with an atlatl could reach speeds of 100 miles per hour (161 kph)!

Native American Peoples
(Before European Contact)

This map shows the general area of Native American peoples before European settlers arrived.

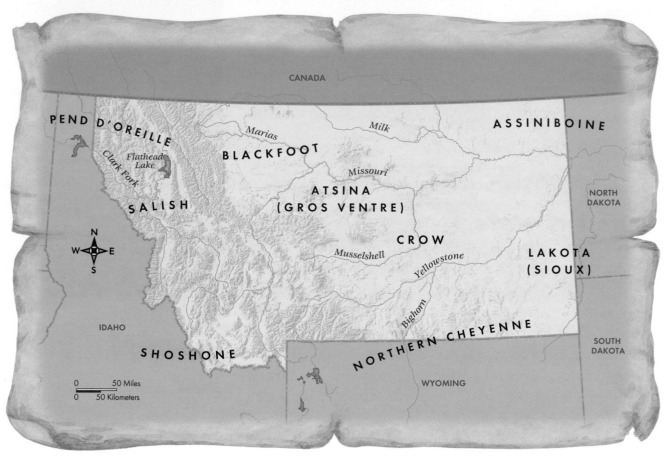

bison was a challenge. A full-grown bison can weigh as much as 2,000 pounds (907 kilograms), and it has thick skin. For short spurts, a bison can run as fast as a horse. Hunters regularly shot arrows into a large bison only to see the animal run off to nurse its wounds far from the reach of people. To more easily kill bison, hunters learned to corner them and force them to run off cliffs. Archaeologists have found great stacks of bones at the bottom of cliffs, which they call buffalo jumps.

The men and women of ancient Montana were great travelers and traders. They built bull boats made of willow frames covered with bison hides, which they used to ply the rivers. For traveling overland, they stretched a frame over a pair of poles to make a sled called a travois. They hitched their dogs to the travois loaded with their possessions. Though the people of the mountains and plains led different lives, they met often to exchange stories and goods.

There were some similarities in the religious beliefs of the Native peoples who lived in what is now Montana. All believed that spirits, which could be good or evil, inhabited the earth. Virtually all early Montanans worshipped a single creator god who was all-powerful and ruled the universe. In rock paintings, the creator god was sometimes drawn as a coyote.

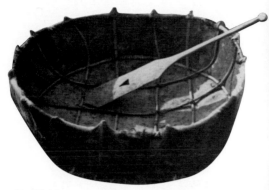
Bull boat

CHANGES FROM AFAR

European people began arriving in North America in the 1500s. First, the Spaniards built an empire far to the south in present-day Mexico. Then the British and the French established colonies along the Atlantic coast.

The people in Montana, which was far inland and surrounded by forbidding mountains and vast plains, were unaware of the arrival of the Europeans. They felt the effects of the foreigners' arrival long before seeing them. As Europeans in the south and the east established settlements and sought trade goods, they disrupted the lives of the Native peoples there, forcing many Native nations to move. This upheaval drove different Native American groups into Montana in the 17th and 18th centuries. As newcomers arrived, the Natives fought for territory. Weaker communities were driven into the mountains or out of Montana entirely.

SEE IT HERE!

PICTOGRAPH CAVE STATE PARK

Pictograph Cave State Park near Billings preserves pictographs, rock paintings drawn by ancient people. For centuries, ancient people sought shelter in what became Pictograph Cave. They painted pictures on the walls using paint made from cherry juice, animal fat, and charcoal. Most pictures in the cave show animals. One drawing depicts a man with a shield.

This engraving shows an Assiniboine encampment, along with dogs pulling travois.

Native Americans did not have horses until the Spaniards introduced them into North America. Horses revolutionized Native American life because they made bison hunting much easier.

The Shoshone people arrived in Montana from the south. Their fighters rode horses that they had acquired from Spaniards. The Shoshones stormed into Montana, driving the Salish people from the plains into the mountains and pushing the Blackfoot people north toward today's Canada. Once the Blackfoot people also acquired horses, guns, and metal arrowheads and spear points, they waged war on Shoshones and reclaimed much of their old territory.

By 1800, Montana was home to dozens of Native American settlements. Many nations had been pushed out of their homes over the previous 100 years by ever-expanding white settlement. The plains were home to the Arapaho, Assiniboine, Atsina, Blackfoot, Northern Cheyenne, and Crow peoples. In the Rocky Mountains lived the Bannock, Salish, Kalispel, and Shoshone peoples. The powerful Lakota Nation lived east of Montana, but they used Montana as a hunting ground.

NATIVE AMERICAN LIFE

The people of Montana's Great Plains lived primarily in cone-shaped tipis. Made up of poles covered by buffalo hides, tipis could be taken down and packed up in less than an hour. Plains people moved often to be near migrating bison herds. Women owned the tipis and had the responsibility of setting up and dismantling them. The women sometimes tied a rattle made out of a gourd with a pebble inside to the tipi entrance. The rattle served as a "doorbell" for anyone wishing to come inside.

People in the Rocky Mountain region also lived in tipis, but they did not move as often. During the winter, many people in the mountains lived in log lodges. Rocky Mountain dwellers were great traders, and they traveled in canoes. Those who grew crops of beans, corn, and squash mostly stayed in one place. Both the mountain and the plains peoples made clothing from deerskin and buffalo hides.

NEWCOMERS ARRIVE

The Native people regarded the first non-Native people who ventured into Montana with curiosity. The newcomers brought interesting trade goods such as iron axes and cooking pots. The first contacts between the two people were largely friendly. No one guessed how quickly and how thoroughly the newcomers would change Native life in Montana.

Picture Yourself . . .

Hunting on Horseback

You are a Blackfoot hunter in the Great Plains region of Montana. You primarily hunt bison, which is difficult because they are so strong and swift. You and your fellow hunters try to stampede the animals off cliffs, but this is not always possible. So you hunt individual buffalo with a bow and arrow. You are skilled with the weapons and extremely patient when stalking animals on foot. Your family depends on you for food, and you do not wish to disappoint them.

One day, a new group of people appears on the plains, bringing with them an animal you've never seen before. It is bigger than a deer and as fast as a buffalo. Best of all, it is tame and actually allows you to ride on its back. It is a horse. Your people trade their most valuable possessions to buy several horses. Now, on horseback, when you head to the plains to hunt, you are the bison's equal. You can chase down the biggest animal in a herd. You realize at once that the horse will change your way of life.

Blackfoot hunters on horseback

READ ABOUT

Explorers were
drawn to the
Rocky Mountains
and the region that
became Montana.

1743

*Frenchmen François
and Louis-Joseph de La
Vérendrye are likely the
first Europeans to set foot
in today's Montana*

1803 ▲

*The Louisiana Purchase
makes most of Montana
U.S. territory*

1805

*The Lewis and Clark
expedition passes through
Montana*

CHAPTER THREE

EXPLORATION AND SETTLEMENT

★

I N 1800, WHAT IS NOW THE NORTH-WESTERN UNITED STATES WAS A WILD REGION WITH EXCITING PROSPECTS. It had staggering mountains, towering trees, rushing rivers, and gleaming lakes. Great Britain, France, Spain, and Russia all laid claim to the Northwest. But it was the young United States that boldly explored the region, encouraged settlement, and finally took control of the area. This region is now the states of Washington, Oregon, Idaho, Wyoming, and Montana.

1807

Fur traders build Fort Lisa, the region's first permanent European structure

1841

Catholic priests establish St. Mary's Mission in the Bitterroot Mountains

1862 ▶

Gold is discovered at Grasshopper Creek, setting off a gold rush

François and Louis-Joseph de La Vérendrye and their crew may have been the first Europeans in Montana.

SEARCHING FOR THE NORTHWEST PASSAGE

For centuries, Europeans dreamed of finding the Northwest Passage, a natural sea route that would allow ships to sail from the Atlantic to the Pacific without going all the way around the southern tip of South America. Europeans had been searching for this imaginary route since Italian explorer Christopher Columbus stumbled on the Americas in late 1492. The quest for the Northwest Passage sparked many explorations in North America.

In the 1700s, France claimed all of what is now Canada. Two French brothers, François and Louis-

Joseph de La Vérendrye, ventured west in 1743, seeking to trade with Native people and find the Northwest Passage. The brothers may have advanced as far as Montana. They claimed they saw "shining mountains" to the west. British explorers also probed the region. British-owned fur-trading companies operated on the Pacific coast, and their scouts explored the inland reaches of the Columbia River.

When the United States won its independence from Great Britain in 1783, its territory extended from the Atlantic Ocean to the Mississippi River. Most of the land beyond the Mississippi was unexplored by Europeans, and European control of that land was in dispute. At various times, Spain and France claimed the western lands, which were called Louisiana. In 1803, President Thomas Jefferson bought Louisiana from France. The sale, called the Louisiana Purchase, doubled the size of the United States overnight. It was the greatest land deal in history.

President Jefferson sent an exploring party into the Louisiana region with orders to seek a water route to the Pacific and to make peaceful contact with Native nations. Jefferson chose his private secretary, Meriwether Lewis, to lead the expedition. Lewis selected his friend William Clark to act as second in command. Lewis and Clark and their exploring party, called the **Corps** of Discovery, plunged into unknown lands and wrote one of the most exciting episodes of U.S. history.

Louisiana Purchase

This map shows the area (in yellow) that made up the Louisiana Purchase and the present-day state of Montana (in orange).

British Possessions

Louisiana Purchase

Spanish Possessions

United States, 1803

Louisiana Purchase

United States Territory, 1803

Present-day state of Montana

W★OW

The Louisiana region eventually became all or part of 15 U.S. states.

WORD TO KNOW

corps *a group working together on a special mission*

Sacagawea, a guide for the Corps of Discovery, is greeted by the Shoshone people.

There are more statues of Sacagawea in the United States than of any other woman.

THE LEWIS AND CLARK EXPEDITION

In May 1804, the Corps of Discovery left St. Louis, Missouri, and pushed west along the Missouri River. After a rugged five-month trip, they made camp with the Mandan people in what is now North Dakota. There they met a French trapper, Toussaint Charbonneau, and his young Shoshone wife, Sacagawea. She would become vital to the expedition as a translator and negotiator with the Native American nations they encountered.

After spending the winter in North Dakota, Lewis and Clark resumed their westward journey in the spring of 1805. On April 26, they came upon the fork where the Yellowstone River branches off from the Missouri. After marching a few miles west, the party entered today's Montana. Lewis called the future state a paradise for its "immense herds" of game animals such as bison, elk, and deer.

On June 13, 1805, while still following the Missouri River, Lewis heard a roaring in the distance. It sounded like tumbling water but was so loud that it made the earth tremble. He walked closer and then stopped "to gaze on this sublimely grand spectacle . . . the grandest sight I ever beheld." Lewis had discovered the Great Falls of the Missouri, the most powerful waterfall he had ever seen.

When the Corps of Discovery reached the Rockies, they met some Shoshones and tried to trade goods for horses. Here Sacagawea proved valuable. She was Shoshone, and by chance the leader who greeted Lewis and Clark was her brother. With Sacagawea's aid, the party bought horses and continued to climb the Rockies. During their journey over the mountains, the men noticed the rivers now flowed west, indicating they had crossed the Continental Divide. Finally, they found a wide, westward-flowing river, the Columbia, and followed it to their destination: the Pacific Ocean.

MINI-BIO

SACAGAWEA: GUIDING LEWIS AND CLARK

Sacagawea (1786?–1812) was born in what is now Idaho. At about age 13, she became the wife of French trapper Toussaint Charbonneau. Lewis and Clark hired Charbonneau as an interpreter, but they never trusted him. Sacagawea, on the other hand, became a valued and well-liked member of the expedition, who helped the corps communicate with the Native people they met. She gave birth to a boy named Jean Baptiste shortly after joining the party, and the men took to the baby, too. Though her year of death is listed as 1812, according to some stories, she lived much longer.

❓ **Want to know more?** See www.pbs.org/lewisandclark/inside/saca.html

THE OREGON TREATY

The Louisiana Purchase brought most of Montana under U.S. control. But the Pacific Northwest, including Montana's Bitterroot Range, did not officially become American until the U.S. and British governments signed the Oregon Treaty in 1846.

FAQ

Q: WHAT HAPPENED TO THE GREAT FALLS?

A: In order to generate electricity, Americans built five dams along the Missouri River near the Great Falls, and the falls have been tamed. The city of Great Falls, located where the falls once roared, is now the third-largest city in Montana. It is called the Electric City because its dams produce so much **hydroelectric power**.

WORD TO KNOW

hydroelectric power *electricity generated by the force of water passing over a dam*

The Lewis and Clark expedition covered some 8,000 miles (12,875 km), from the Mississippi to the Pacific Coast and back. Most of the journey took place in what is now Montana. Following Jefferson's orders, the party forged friendly relations with Native American groups, except for the Blackfoot people, who did not trust them because they had befriended their enemies. The Corps of Discovery was unable to find the Northwest Passage, however. The expedition seemed to dash any hopes that the sea passage existed.

MINI-BIO

YORK: ON THE TRAIL WITH LEWIS AND CLARK

York (c. 1770—c. 1831), an enslaved African who had been William Clark's companion since childhood, was the first person of African descent to set foot in what would become Montana. He played an important role in the Lewis and Clark expedition. He was a skilled hunter, fisher, and negotiator, often working with Sacagawea. York shared the same duties and took the same risks as the other men. He and Sacagawea earned the right to vote on important issues that the explorers faced. At the end of the two-and-a-half-year journey so vital to the country, York asked Clark for his freedom. Years later, William Clark claimed he had freed York, but no one knows for certain.

 Want to know more? See www.pbs.org/lewisandclark/inside/york.html

TRAPPERS AND TRADERS

Not long after Lewis and Clark passed through Montana, fur trappers and traders entered Montana seeking riches. The fur of beavers and otters was made into hats and scarves and sold for high prices in eastern states. It could be said that fur was the Treasure State's first treasure.

Lewis and Clark had reported that streams in Montana swarmed with beavers and other fur-bearing animals. This stirred excitement in the frontier outpost town of St. Louis. The first St. Louis fur trader who set out for Montana was Manuel Lisa, a tough and experienced frontiersman. His guide was George Drouillard, a veteran of the Lewis and Clark expedition. In November 1807, Lisa and his party set up a trading post where the Yellowstone and Bighorn rivers meet. The fort came to be called Fort Lisa, and it was the first permanent structure built by white settlers in Montana.

Fort Benton was built along the Missouri River as a fur-trading post.

SEE IT HERE!

POMPEYS PILLAR NATIONAL MONUMENT

On the return trip along the Yellowstone River, William Clark spotted a 200-foot (61 m) cliff near present-day Billings and stopped long enough to carve his name and the date, July 25, 1806, on the cliff side. More than 200 years later, you can still see Clark's carving on the rocky surface. Clark called the cliff Pomp's Tower after Sacagawea's baby, whom he had nicknamed Little Pomp, meaning "little chief." Today, the cliff, which also has Native American drawings on it, is a national monument.

Exploration of Montana

The colored arrows on this map show the routes taken by explorers between 1805 and 1808.

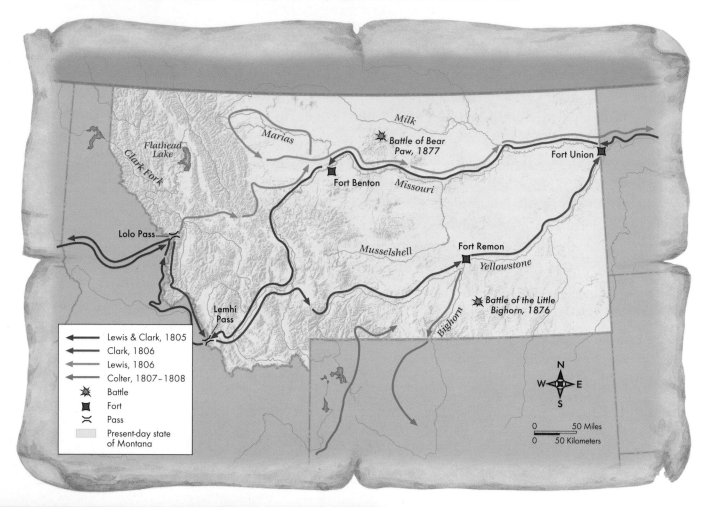

Legend:
- Lewis & Clark, 1805
- Clark, 1806
- Lewis, 1806
- Colter, 1807–1808
- ✷ Battle
- ▮ Fort
- ⋊ Pass
- Present-day state of Montana

THE MOUNTAIN MEN

The hardy trappers who ventured into the Rocky Mountains after Lewis and Clark were called mountain men. They lived and worked alone for months at a time, trapping animals and storing their pelts. They learned Native languages, and many married Native women. These rugged mountain men included Kit Carson, John Colter, Jim Bridger, and African American trappers James Beckwourth and Edward Rose.

The fur business was profitable for those who got to Montana early. Groups of trappers formed companies and built forts and trading posts along Montana's riverbanks. In 1822, one company shipped $25,000 worth of pelts to eastern markets. At that time, $25,000 was a small fortune.

Throughout the region, bison were hunted almost to extinction.

The fur trade had some tragic consequences. In less than 30 years, beavers and otters, once so numerous in Montana, had been dramatically reduced through trapping. Hunters next turned to bison, because their hides were also worth money in the East. They shot and skinned the bison, then left their meat to rot on the ground. "Sportsmen hunters" also took their toll. In 1854, a wealthy Irishman named George Gore hunted along the Yellowstone River and bragged that he killed 2,000 bison, 1,600 deer, and 100 bears. Killing bison for fun or for profit was a tragedy not only for the animals but also to the Native Americans who had relied on them for centuries as a source of food, shelter, and clothing.

The fur trade also brought disease to Native Americans in Montana. White traders unknowingly carried smallpox, diphtheria, and other diseases to the Montana wilderness. These diseases had long been common in Europe. Because of this, Europeans had

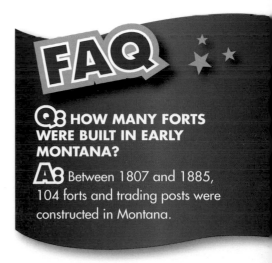

FAQ

Q: HOW MANY FORTS WERE BUILT IN EARLY MONTANA?

A: Between 1807 and 1885, 104 forts and trading posts were constructed in Montana.

A view of St. Mary's Mission in the Bitterroot Valley, 1840s

WORDS TO KNOW

immunity *a body's ability to resist disease*

mission *a place created by a religious group to spread its beliefs*

acquired an **immunity**, so that the illnesses would make them sick but would seldom kill them. Native Americans had never come into contact with these diseases before, so they had no such immunities. The diseases swept through communities after Indians met whites in North America, killing huge numbers of people. Smallpox devastated the Blackfoot people of Montana in the 1830s and killed half of them.

Catholic priests tried to bring their religion to Montana during the fur-trapping era. In 1841, Father Pierre-Jean De Smet left St. Louis, journeyed west with several other priests, and built a cabin in Montana's Bitterroot Range. The priests called the cabin St. Mary's **Mission**, and it was Montana's first mission church. The priests enjoyed some success, particularly with the Salish people who lived in the Bitterroots. Hundreds of Salishes converted to Christianity.

GOLD!

In 1848, a worker in California saw a sparkling object in a streambed. He reached down and picked up a nugget of gold. That speck, no bigger than a kernel of corn, started a human stampede called the California Gold Rush. Gold seekers raced west. In a little over one year, the population of California swelled from 20,000 to 400,000.

The California Gold Rush planted the dream among Americans that the West held vast riches. Few white Americans moved to Montana until gold was discovered there, too. Then the Land of Shining Mountains experienced its own boom.

Historians disagree as to who first found gold in Montana and exactly when and where it was discovered. Brothers James and Granville Stuart insisted that they were first when they began digging in Montana's Deer Lodge Valley in 1857.

In 1862, a rich goldfield was discovered at Grasshopper Creek in southwestern Montana. Almost overnight, a town called Bannack was born as excited gold seekers flocked in. Bannack was Montana's first boom-and-bust city. Many more such towns would appear out of nowhere when a mining strike was made and then vanish when the mine had been emptied out.

Prospectors came to Montana from everywhere. Many were "tenderfeet," newcomers who arrived directly from eastern states. Others were veterans of the California goldfields. All rushed to Montana with hopes as high as the big sky itself. By 1866, Montana's non-Indian population was more than 20,000. And Montana was the country's second-largest gold producer, trailing only California. Mining ushered in a new era for the Treasure State.

Picture Yourself...

as a Teenage Prospector in Montana

The news has spread across the nation. Gold has been discovered in Montana! Your family agrees to pay for the expensive trip out west. You make your way to Montana mostly on foot, although part of the journey is on river rafts. In the goldfields, you are among older men, some of whom are thieves and even murderers. You learn how to pan for gold dust by holding a pan in a stream. It is frustrating work, performed standing bent over in near-freezing water up to your knees. Chances are you will find very little gold. But you get to see the Montana wilderness and that is a thrill you will remember for the rest of your life.

Pan and gold nuggets

WORD TO KNOW

prospectors *people who search a region for valuable minerals*

READ ABOUT

Workers with pickaxes and shovels at the entrance of a Montana mine, 1880s

1864

The Montana Territory is established

1870

U.S. troops massacre 173 Blackfoot people on the Marias River

▲**1876**

Native forces defeat U.S. troops at the Battle of the Little Bighorn

CHAPTER FOUR

GROWTH AND CHANGE

★

PROSPECTORS CAME TO MONTANA IN SEARCH OF GOLD AND SILVER. For many years, Montana was a dangerous place where men settled arguments with fists and guns. Eventually, mining gave way to farming and ranching. By the early 1900s, the Wild West era was over and the new state of Montana faced a bright future.

1880–90
Settlers pour into Montana, increasing the population fivefold

1883 ▲
The Northern Pacific Railway, running the length of Montana, is completed

1886
Drought and freezing weather almost destroy Montana's cattle industry

After the discovery of gold, Helena grew into a bustling city.

Q8 WHAT EXACTLY IS A TERRITORY?

A8 A territory is a political unit controlled by the federal government. It has a governor and a legislature. In the 1800s, becoming a territory was the first step for a region toward achieving statehood.

BECOMING A TERRITORY

On May 26, 1864, President Abraham Lincoln signed documents officially establishing Montana as a territory. At the time, the Civil War (1861–1865) was raging in the eastern United States, but the fierce fighting between Confederate and Union soldiers never approached the isolated Montana Territory.

The Montana Territory was created out of the existing Idaho Territory. The mining boomtown of Bannack served as the territorial capital. True to the boom-and-bust nature of the times, Bannack thrived for a decade or two but was all but abandoned in less than 30 years.

Virginia City, another mining boomtown, grew to a population of 10,000 within a year of when gold was discovered there in 1863. In 1865, it became the new territorial capital, but after the gold ran out, its population also dwindled.

THE MINING FRONTIER

One of Montana's early gold strikes was made at Confederate Gulch near present-day Townsend. The place got its name in 1864 when four former Confederate soldiers found gold deposits in a streambed. The stream was so rich it was said a miner panning there could pick out $1,000 in gold dust in just one hour.

A boomtown called Diamond City grew almost overnight at the site, and the town reached a population of 10,000 people. Many Diamond City residents had been Civil War soldiers on either the Union and the Confederate sides. Some had run away from their army units and traveled to the Montana Territory to escape punishment. The former Union and Confederate soldiers took their wartime hatreds with them to Montana, and this alone caused many arguments and bloody fights.

"Claim jumping" caused many clashes among miners. When a miner or a group of miners discovered gold, they were required to register their find at a claims office run by the territorial government. A claim issued by the office meant that no one other than the claim holders was allowed to search for gold at that particular spot. But there were no police departments or officials on hand to enforce this policy. Sometimes claim jumpers would mine on land where other people held claims. If miners wanted to protect a claim, they had to fight claim jumpers themselves.

The center of violence in territorial times was Bannack, the capital city. Unlike many boomtowns, Bannack had a sheriff and a city government. But the sheriff, Henry Plummer, was one of the most cold-hearted criminals in the entire territory. Plummer came from the California goldfields, where he was known as a thief and a murderer. He was also handsome, well

The diggings at Confederate Gulch produced between $10 million and $30 million worth of gold in just a few years.

READ AND REFLECT!

In view of the fact that CRIME has run riot to such an alarming extent in the Territory of Montana, (particularly East of the Missouri River,) during the past six months, and that

Murders AND High-handed Outrages

Have been of such frequent occurrence as to excite the just indignation of all good citizens, it is believed that it is now time that the GOOD WORK should be re-commenced. Therefore,

THIS IS TO NOTIFY ALL WHOM IT MAY CONCERN!

That CRIME MUST AND WILL BE SUPPRESSED! and to that end, all OFFENDERS

WILL BE SUMMARILY DEALT WITH!

AND PUNISHED AS OF OLD!

BY ORDER OF

VIGILANCE COMMITTEE.

A notice from Montana's Vigilance Committee, 1860

WORD TO KNOW

vigilantes *volunteers who try on their own to stop crime and punish criminals*

dressed, and gentlemanly. He used his charm to get elected sheriff of Bannack. Once in office, he began a reign of terror. Plummer hired a gang of deputies, most of whom had criminal backgrounds. Between 1862 and 1864, Plummer and his crew robbed countless miners of their gold.

Violent crime in the territory triggered the rise of **vigilantes**. Meeting in secret, vigilantes formed armies that sometimes numbered as many as 2,000 men. Their declared purpose was to bring law to the Montana mining frontier, but vigilantes often used lawless methods to enforce their will. In January 1864, a group of vigilantes arrested Henry Plummer and hanged him without a trial. Several other members of Plummer's crew were given quick trials before they, too, were hanged.

Frontier violence and the fight put up by vigilantes is often made to seem heroic in books and movies. In reality, the mining frontier was a grim period in Montana history, a time when people lived in fear.

GROWING TOWNS

In 1870 in Helena, men outnumbered women three to one. Other Montana towns were also home to many more men than women. Gradually, women and children arrived, and over time, the nature of Montana's mining camps changed. Churches and schools were built. Regular Methodist services were held in Bannack as early as 1864. An 1868 government report said 704 children attended 25 public schools scattered throughout the territory.

The journey taken by most newcomers to Montana required both steamboat and stagecoach travel. Steamboats regularly left St. Louis and chugged up the Missouri River as far as Fort Benton in north-central Montana. In 1867 alone, some 10,000 passengers arrived at Fort Benton. From there, they took stagecoaches and horse-drawn wagons or they walked to the growing communities of Great Falls, Helena, Butte, Virginia City, and Missoula.

Over time, mining changed in Montana. No longer did individuals own mines. Instead, companies owned them. The companies employed their own police forces, which put an end to battles over claim jumping. By the time the big companies moved in, all the gold that was easy to mine had already been taken from Montana. The gold that remained required industrial methods to extract it from the ground. As the amount of gold being unearthed dropped, mining companies turned their attention to silver and later to copper.

The people of early Montana felt so isolated that they spoke as if they lived in a foreign land, calling the rest of the country "the States."

SEE IT HERE!

GHOST TOWNS

As the gold ran out, many mining settlements were abandoned. They became ghost towns, once-thriving cities that now held nothing but rows of empty houses, streets, and stores. Montana has at least 22 ghost towns, including Bannack, once the territorial capital. Visitors to Bannack walk the silent streets and imagine life as it was more than a century ago during the mining boom.

People from eastern states as well as Europe found work in the Montana Territory.

GROWING DIVERSITY

Many people who moved to Montana were from eastern states, and many others were from Europe. Twenty languages were spoken in the town of Helena alone, and nearly half the men in the territory had been born abroad.

Although they were few in number, some African Americans managed to reach Montana's gold mines and strike it rich. In 1869, James Pratt discovered gold in Marysville. He then moved to Helena, where he owned a saloon. Millie Ringgold, who had once been enslaved in Maryland, dug up $1,800 worth of gold and started a hotel and restaurant. Some black settlers chose to ignore gold for other matters. William Briarpaugh was only 21 when he began a farm in Cascade County that became one of the largest wheat ranches in Montana. From 1888 to 1931, Sarah Gammon Bickford owned the

Virginia City Water Company, which supplied water to the entire city.

Some African Americans moved to Montana to escape **discrimination** in the East, but they often encountered **segregation** in the new territory. In 1872, the territorial government required that separate schools be built for black and white children. By 1883, the legislature had given up on the idea of segregated schools, in part because it was too expensive to build two schools when one would do.

By 1900, African Americans in Helena had established their own churches, literary societies, women's clubs, and a theatrical troupe for community entertainment. Two African American newspapers, the *Helena Colored Citizen* and the *Montana Plaindealer*, flourished by providing important information to readers and denouncing discrimination. African American women started the Afro-American Building Association to promote real estate and business among African Americans. Three of its eight managers were women.

Hundreds of Chinese people settled in the Montana Territory during the mining boom. Many moved from California, where they had worked in the goldfields or on the railroad. In Montana, many Chinese settlers took jobs in laundries or worked as servants for the well-to-do. By 1900, most Chinese had left Montana.

Native Americans were the largest nonwhite group in the Montana Territory. As more white settlers arrived, the U.S. government forced Native Americans onto reservations. To Native Americans, especially those in the eastern plains, being crowded onto reservations was a devastating assault on their way of life. For generations, Plains people had followed herds of bison across the open land. But reservations had boundaries, and Native

WORDS TO KNOW

discrimination *unequal treatment based on race, gender, religion, or other factors*

segregation *separation from others, according to race, class, ethnic group, religion, or other factors*

MINI-BIO

PLENTY COUPS: CROW LEADER

Plenty Coups (1848–1932) was a Crow leader who tried to help his people peacefully accept their white neighbors and adapt to the reservation life that was forced upon them. Yet he insisted that Crows honor their old arts, customs, and traditions. Mostly he urged the young to go to school because an education opened broad opportunities. His name is a translation of the Crow word *alaxchiiaahush*, meaning "many achievements." In 1884, he built a home that is today the centerpiece of Chief Plenty Coups State Park on the Crow Indian Reservation.

 Want to know more? See http://montanakids.com/cool_stories/Famous_Montanans/coups.htm

WORD TO KNOW

cavalry *soldiers who ride on horseback*

hunters were forbidden to cross them. The U.S. Army enforced the boundaries by building forts on the frontier and manning them with **cavalry** troops.

Despite the presence of the army, clashes broke out between Native Americans and white settlers. Many Blackfoot people resisted white encroachment on their shrinking territory. A leader known as Mountain Chief led an aggressive group of Blackfoot people. But a man called Heavy Runner led a peaceful group. Major Eugene Baker of the U.S. Army mistrusted all the Blackfoot people. On January 23, 1870, troops led by Baker attacked Heavy Runner's Blackfoot village, slaughtering 173 people. Most of the Blackfoot men were away hunting, so many of the dead were elderly people, women, and children. This bloody attack is known as the Baker Massacre.

THE LAST STAND

The most powerful group of Plains Indians were the Lakota people. They regarded the Black Hills of South Dakota as sacred land, a place where the souls of their ancestors lived. In 1875, a gold strike brought hundreds of white prospectors to the Black Hills. This invasion violated a treaty the government had signed giving the Black Hills to the Lakota Nation for "as long as the

Buffalo Soldiers at Fort Shaw

rivers shall run and the grass shall grow." Ignoring this promise, the U.S. government sent troops to protect the prospectors in the Black Hills.

The Lakota people, furious over the betrayal by the U.S. government, rallied behind their spiritual leader Sitting Bull (c. 1831–1890). During a ritual called the Sun Dance, which required participants to shun food and water and pierce themselves with pins, Sitting Bull had a vision in which he saw white soldiers and their horses falling upside down into the Lakota camp. After that, he led a large fighting force west into the Montana Territory. He was joined by another Lakota leader, named Crazy Horse, and many Northern Cheyenne and Arapaho forces. They were ready for war.

BUFFALO SOLDIERS

Several forts in Montana were manned by African Americans of the Ninth Cavalry Regiment, whom Native Americans called Buffalo Soldiers. Buffalo were sacred to Native Americans, and they may have called the Ninth Cavalry Buffalo Soldiers out of respect for their courage and fighting ability. The Buffalo Soldiers guarded wagon routes and settlement towns, helping to preserve peace in early Montana.

SEE IT HERE!

CUSTER'S LAST STAND

The Little Bighorn Battlefield National Monument is a 765-acre (310 ha) park located south of the town of Hardin. The park honors the cavalrymen and the Native Americans who died there in 1876. Park visitors are drawn to Last Stand Hill, where tombstones mark the spots where individual cavalrymen died. The Little Bighorn Battlefield National Monument is one of the most popular tourist attractions in Montana.

Into the Montana Territory rode the Seventh Cavalry Regiment, under the command of Lieutenant Colonel George Armstrong Custer. During the Civil War, Custer had boldly led cavalry charges against the enemy. He had a reputation as a "glory hunter," an officer who fought recklessly in battle in order to gain newspaper headlines trumpeting his bravery.

On June 25, 1876, Custer's scouts spotted the Lakota camp along the Little Bighorn River in the Montana Territory. Custer had expected to clash with only a few hundred Native Americans, but instead 2,500 to 5,000 Native forces—including Lakota, Northern Cheyenne, and Arapaho—had gathered on the riverbank. Custer then made a series of decisions that historians have questioned ever since. First, he divided his regiment into three groups. Next, he called for an immediate attack by the group he commanded, even though his men were outnumbered ten to one.

After much bloody fighting, the troops led by Custer retreated to a hillside, where Native American fighters surrounded them. Custer's troops were overwhelmed. All the soldiers under Custer's immediate command—about 225 men—were killed. Among those who died was Isaiah Dorman, an African American who was married to a Lakota woman and had been hired by Custer as an interpreter. It was a terrible defeat for the U.S cavalry.

Still, newspaper reports hailed Custer as a hero. Artists imagined the battle scene and portrayed Custer standing in the middle of his troops bravely defending his ground. The Battle of the Little Bighorn came to be called Custer's Last Stand. Actually, the Little Bighorn clash could be thought of as the last stand for the Plains Indians. Immediately after the battle, U.S. cavalry units began pursuing Sitting Bull and Crazy Horse. Sitting

George Armstrong Custer and his men are surrounded and killed at the Battle of the Little Bighorn in 1876.

Bull and his followers fled to Canada. Most Plains Indians returned to their reservations. Never again would Native Americans in the United States assemble and fight U.S. forces in a major battle.

THE DEVELOPMENT OF EASTERN MONTANA

The mining boom took place in the mountainous western part of the Montana Territory. The plains to the east remained home to only a few settlers. A traveler named Granville Stuart rode through the region and noted, "In 1880 [central Montana] was practically uninhabited. . . . Thousands of buffalo darkened the rolling plains. There were deer, antelope, elk, wolves, and coyotes on every hill." In the fall of 1883, he rode over the same region and noted that, "there was not one buffalo remaining on the range and the antelope, elk, and deer were indeed scarce."

In just a few short years, Montana's plains had changed dramatically. Hunters destroyed the bison in order to sell their hides. Some even tried to eliminate the bison entirely in order to weaken the Native American people who relied on them. They hoped this would force the Native Americans to stay on their reservations and accept government **rations** as food.

Cattle owners who dreamed of earning a fortune from their animals moved into this open range. Many were experienced cattlemen from Texas. Each branded his cattle with his own special mark and let them roam on the vast grasslands of eastern Montana. When the owners wanted to round up their cattle, they would look for the brands. Cattle owners commonly kept herds numbering more than 1,000 head. The Montana economy had entered yet another stage, having evolved from fur trapping to mining to cattle raising.

Cattle replaced wild buffalo on the grasslands of eastern Montana, but they were very different types of animals. The hardy bison could endure cold winters and dry summers. Cattle were less able to survive the harsh and unpredictable weather. The summer of 1886 was hot and dry, yet cattlemen brought still more animals onto the plains. Territorial Governor Samuel T. Hauser cautioned against adding more cattle saying, "Our ranges are already bare." Then came the disastrous winter of 1886–87, when snow covered the grasses, and icy winds swept over the plains. Huge numbers

WORD TO KNOW

rations *food allowances from a given supply*

By 1900, Montana had 6 million head of sheep. They outnumbered people 24 to one.

of cattle died, perhaps as many as 360,000 head, more than half of the territory's entire stock.

Following Montana's harsh winter of 1886–87, many ranchers chose to raise smaller herds of cattle.

The terrible drought and freeze brought a quick end to Montana's cattle boom period. Ranchers continued to raise cattle in Montana, but they kept much smaller herds than in the past. Many ranchers turned to raising sheep because sheep are hardier and better able to survive freezing winters and drought.

THE RAILROAD ARRIVES

Railroads transformed the Montana Territory. The first transcontinental railroad, which connected Chicago, Illinois, with Sacramento, California, was completed in 1869, but that railroad ran far south of the Montana Territory. Montana settlers needed a railroad passing through it to bring in new settlers.

56

Some 1,500 Chinese laborers helped build the Northern Pacific Railway.

LAND AND RAILROAD DEVELOPMENT

To encourage the building of railroads, the federal government gave enormous tracts of land to railroad companies. The land grants amounted to far more than just the ground alongside the railroad tracks. The government gave the Northern Pacific 17 million acres (6.9 million ha) in the Montana Territory. The company was free to sell this land. The Northern Pacific became the second-largest landowner in Montana, behind only the federal government.

In 1881, money was raised and plans were made to build the Northern Pacific Railway. The aim of the Northern Pacific was to link Seattle, Washington, to Chicago. The rails would run through the center of Montana. Northern Pacific's crews laid track from both the east and the west. The two crews met at the town of Gold Creek, Montana, on September 8, 1883. A great party, attended by former U.S. president Ulysses Grant, was held at Gold Creek as officials drove in the last spike completing the long stretch of track. At last, Montana had a railroad running the length of the state. Goods and settlers could now be brought by rail to once-isolated towns such as Missoula, Bozeman, and Helena.

In April 1887, construction began on the Great Northern Railway. This railroad was designed to run along the northern border with Canada and bring the wealth of Montana's mines east to processing plants in the Great Lakes region. An aggressive businessman named James Hill directed the Great Northern. A Canadian by birth, Hill was nicknamed the Empire Builder for his ability to transform lands in the American West by building railroads. When building the Great Northern in Montana, Hill ran into a problem: much of the land that the railroad would pass through had been promised to Native American nations for use as reservations. Hill convinced Congress to strip the land from the Native Americans and grant it to Hill's railroad. The Great Northern opened for business in 1893. New towns such as Havre, Kalispell, and Columbia Falls appeared along the rails, built almost overnight.

As the railroads were being built, more and more people moved to the territory. It would soon be accepted as a state.

MINI-BIO

MARY FIELDS: STAGECOACH MARY

Mary Fields (1832–1914) arrived in Montana from Ohio in 1884 to work in a Catholic mission near the town of Cascade. The 6-foot-tall (183 cm) African American was a skilled shooter. After 10 years at the mission, she lost her job when she got into a gunfight with a white cowhand. By this time, she was about 60 years old, but she soon found work driving a stagecoach to deliver mail to remote homes. This made her the second woman and the first African American woman to work for the U.S. Postal Service. Fields always delivered the mail on time, no matter what the weather, and she became known as Stagecoach Mary because of her dedication to the job.

? **Want to know more?** See www.lkwdpl.org/WIHOHIO/fiel-mar.htm

WOW

Largely because of railroad development, the population of the Montana Territory increased fivefold from 1880 to 1890.

The preamble to
the 1884 Montana
Constitution

~ Constitution ~

~ of the ~

State of Montana.

Preamble.

The object of the institution, maintenance and administration of government, is to secure the existence of the body politic, to protect it, and to furnish the individuals who compose it, with the power of enjoying in safety and tranquility their natural rights and the blessings of life; and whenever these great objects are not obtained, the people have a right to alter or change their form of government, and to take measures necessary for their safety, prosperity and happiness.

The body politic is formed by a voluntary association of individuals; it is a social compact by which the whole people covenant with each citizen and each citizen with the whole people, that all should be governed by certain laws for the common good.

It is the duty of the people, therefore, in framing a constitution of government to pre-

1880s
*Copper mining brings
great wealth to Montana*

▲**1889**
*Montana becomes the
41st state in the Union*

1914
*Women in Montana
win the right to vote*

CHAPTER FIVE

MORE MODERN TIMES

★

IN 1884, MONTANA APPLIED FOR STATEHOOD BUT WAS DENIED. And politics played a part in this. Voters in early Montana tended to support Democrats. Republicans, who were in the majority in Washington, were reluctant to admit a Democratic state and thus weaken their own party. North Dakota, South Dakota, and Washington were denied statehood for similar reasons. But all that would soon change.

1916 ►

Jeannette Rankin of Missoula becomes the first woman elected to the U.S. Congress

1973

Montana passes a law requiring that land damaged by mining be returned to its natural state

21st century

Tourism flourishes in Montana

MINI-BIO

JOSEPH KEMP TOOLE: MONTANA'S FIRST GOVERNOR

Joseph Kemp Toole (1851–1929) was born in Savannah, Missouri, and came to the Montana Territory when he was 18. Toole settled in Helena, then a frontier outpost only five years old. He practiced law and held local offices. He was a member of the 1889 constitutional convention, which wrote the document that led to statehood. A Democrat, he was well-liked by most political leaders regardless of their parties. Toole served as governor from 1889 to 1893 and again from 1901 to 1908.

 Want to know more? See www.montanacapitol.com/exhibits/governorsreception/pdf/toole.pdf

When Montana became a state in 1889, only 15 percent of its roughly 140,000 people had been born within its borders.

STATEHOOD

In early 1889, Congress passed an act that guaranteed western states admission to the Union if they had proper constitutions. So in July of that year, a group of Montanans met at a convention in Helena to write up a constitution and to reapply for statehood. The members of the convention represented many different groups. They were Democrats as well as Republicans. Some members of the convention served mining interests while others were loyal to ranchers. Finally, after much arguing, the members of the convention worked out a constitution for their future state.

On November 8, 1889, Montana was accepted as America's 41st state. Joseph K. Toole served as the state's first governor, and Helena was chosen as the capital city.

THE COPPER KINGS

Copper was the leading product in Montana. Copper mining was concentrated in Butte, sometimes called the Richest Hill on Earth. Many of the miners who did the hard work of digging for ore were immigrants. Butte had a Finntown (where workers from Finland lived), a Dublin Gulch (a district named after the capital of Ireland), and a Chinatown. The miners worked long hours in filthy conditions for little pay. The air over Butte was often filled with foul-smelling smoke.

Montana: From Territory to Statehood

(1864–1889)

This map shows U.S. territories and the area (in yellow) that became the state of Montana in 1889.

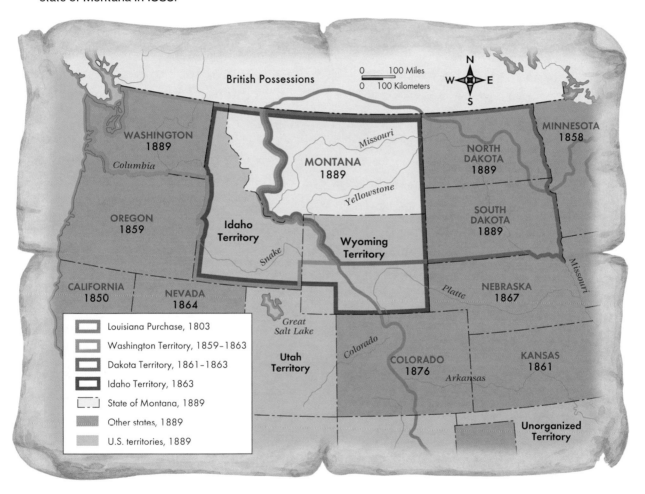

Legend:
- Louisiana Purchase, 1803
- Washington Territory, 1859–1863
- Dakota Territory, 1861–1863
- Idaho Territory, 1863
- State of Montana, 1889
- Other states, 1889
- U.S. territories, 1889

British Possessions

0   100 Miles
0   100 Kilometers

N
W — E
S

WASHINGTON 1889

OREGON 1859

CALIFORNIA 1850

NEVADA 1864

Idaho Territory

Utah Territory

Great Salt Lake

MONTANA 1889

Wyoming Territory

COLORADO 1876

Columbia

Missouri

Yellowstone

Snake

Colorado

Arkansas

Platte

Missouri

NORTH DAKOTA 1889

SOUTH DAKOTA 1889

NEBRASKA 1867

KANSAS 1861

MINNESOTA 1858

Unorganized Territory

Some men became fabulously rich running companies that dug copper from the ground. Called copper kings, these wealthy mine owners gained great political power within the state. The copper kings included William A. Clark, Marcus Daly, and F. Augustus Heinze.

In 1888, Helena was home to as many as 50 millionaires, more millionaires per capita than anywhere else in the world.

MINI-BIO

WILLIAM A. CLARK: MINING TYCOON

William A. Clark (1839–1925) was born in Pennsylvania and arrived in the Montana Territory in 1863 during the height of the mining boom. His early efforts at mining earned him little money, so he branched out into banking and store-keeping. But he always invested his profits in mines, his original love. As copper became more valuable, Clark's holdings made him one of the richest men alive. Although he was worth a fortune, he paid his miners only $3.50 a day. He was an influential man in Montana, but he was not popular with the people. The writer Mark Twain met Clark at a dinner and said of him, "He is as rotten a human being as can be found anywhere on earth."

 Want to know more? See www.pbs.org/wgbh/amex/lasvegas/peopleevents/p_clark.html

FAQ

Q8 WHAT MADE COPPER SUCH A VALUABLE METAL?

A8 Copper was a major component used in making electric wire. The electrical industry boomed in the late 1800s and early 1900s as homes got electricity and household appliances. Montana mines provided the copper for the wire.

William Clark wanted to run for the U.S. Senate in 1899, but Marcus Daly, his rival, opposed him. Daly owned several newspapers, one of which accused Clark of bribing Montana politicians. Clark won the election in 1899, but after he took office, the Senate **censured** him because of the bribery scandal.

Marcus Daly had been born in Ireland. After moving to the United States as a teenager with little money, he worked in California mines before coming to Montana in 1876. Digging near Anaconda, west of Butte, in 1882, Daly's crews discovered a rich vein of copper. Keeping his find a secret, Daly bought up neighboring mines for low prices. In 1883 and 1884, he and several partners built a copper-processing plant at Anaconda, which quickly became the largest in the world. Daly was enormously proud of the town he founded, and he built many elegant buildings that still stand in Anaconda.

WORD TO KNOW

censured *officially blamed or disapproved*

Copper mines near the city of Butte

The newcomer among the copper kings was F. Augustus Heinze, who was born into a wealthy German family in New York City and arrived in Montana in the late 1880s. Heinze was a lawyer who concentrated on mining law. The laws allowed a mine owner to follow an underground vein of metal even if that vein encroached on a neighboring mine. Heinze was a clever performer in court, and he won many cases for mining companies and soon amassed a fortune.

The copper kings battled over which town should serve as state capital. Daly wanted the capital to shift from Helena to Anaconda. Clark denounced the idea, saying that Anaconda was little more than a company town and that Daly owned its only company. Both Daly and Clark spent thousands of dollars to rally voters to their sides. In the end, Helena remained the capital of Montana.

WOW

At one point, Daly wanted to call Anaconda "Copperopolis," but state leaders rejected that name.

The era of the copper kings lasted until the early 1900s when, one by one, the kings sold their holdings to a single, giant corporation largely owned by out-of-state investors such as the wealthy Rockefeller family of New York. That corporation came to be known as the Anaconda Copper Mining Company, and for years it dominated the world market for copper production. It was so big that people in the copper business often referred to Anaconda as simply "the Company." Everyone knew exactly which company was meant.

THE PROGRESSIVE ERA

In the United States, the beginning of the 20th century is called the **Progressive** Era. It was a time when workers and farmers demanded their state governments help poor and working people. The Montana legislature responded by passing a series of progressive laws. In 1904, a Montana law set 16 as the minimum age for anyone to work in mines, and three years later the state made 16 the minimum age for anyone work-

WORD TO KNOW

progressive *making social improvement through government action*

A member of the Montana Federation of Women's Clubs teaching Native Americans to read and write English, 1920s

ing in industry. Montana Progressives won other victories such as limiting the workday to eight hours and regulating mines to make them safer.

Securing voting rights for women was one of the major progressive issues of the early 1900s. In 1914, women in Montana won the right to vote. The Treasure State was one of the first states to give women the vote. Female voting rights extended only to state offices, however. Women were also making progress as officeholders. In 1916, Montanan Jeannette Rankin became the first woman elected to the U.S. House of Representatives.

WAR AND STRIFE

World War I began in Europe in 1914. The leading combatants were Germany and Austria-Hungary on one side and Great Britain and France on the other. The United States joined in when it declared war on Germany in 1917. This ushered in a grim period for Montanans. Almost 40,000 Montanans served in the armed forces during the war, and 939 of them were killed. The war bred fear and mistrust at home. At the height of the conflict, the Montana

MINI-BIO

JEANNETTE RANKIN: CONGRESSIONAL PIONEER

Jeannette Rankin (1880–1973) was born in Missoula, the daughter of ranchers. She was a leader in the 1914 campaign to bring voting rights to Montana women. In 1916, she was elected to the U.S. House of Representatives, becoming the first woman to serve in Congress. A few months later, she was one of only 50 congresspeople who voted against the United States declaring war on Germany and entering World War I. She lost her reelection bid the following year. Rankin was again elected to Congress in 1940. After the Japanese attack on Pearl Harbor, Hawai'i, in 1941, she was the only member of Congress who did not support the declaration of war against Japan, which brought the United States into World War II. Rankin continued her antiwar activity late in life. In 1968, at age 88, she led 5,000 people on a march against U.S. involvement in the Vietnam War.

 Want to know more? See www.greatwomen.org/women.php?action=viewone&id=121

WOW

As of 2008, Jeannette Rankin remained the only woman from Montana ever elected to the U.S. House of Representatives or the U.S. Senate.

UNITED WE STAND

UNLAWFUL
T ON THE
OOR

This is a photograph of a 1942 miners' union meeting in Butte. These organizations had gained strength soon after World War I.

government passed laws that called for jail terms for anyone who spoke out against the war. Some people suspected that German immigrants were spies. Labor unions, which fought for better wages and working conditions for miners, were accused of disrupting the war effort.

One labor leader who hoped to inspire Montana workers was Frank Little. He was an organizer for the Industrial Workers of the World (IWW), a labor union that argued that workers should rule the country. Few details are known about Little's background, except that his mother was Native American. He was tough and fearless. He believed strongly in rights for workers and in the right of free speech for everyone. During rallies, he spoke out against America's entry into World War I, even though he knew this was a dangerous stand. On the night of August 1, 1917, men entered the Butte boardinghouse where Little slept, dragged him out to the street, beat him severely, and then hanged him outside of town. Pinned to Little's body was a note that said, "Others take notice! First and last warning!" Many believed that hired thugs working for the Anaconda Mining Company committed the murder, but no one was ever brought to trial.

World War I ended in 1918, and a time of prosperity called the Roaring Twenties began. Certainly not all Montanans benefited from the good times. Farm prices dropped sharply, and many wheat farmers in the eastern part of the state were forced to sell their holdings. Labor strikes, which sometimes seemed more like wars, rocked the mines and lumber camps. The IWW tried to form a union among Anaconda workers. On April 21, 1920, a gunfight broke out between IWW members and company security guards, who killed two workers.

Frank Little

FARMING GROWTH AND TROUBLE

The number of Montana farms doubled between 1900 and 1910. Most farmers came from other states and settled on the plains of eastern Montana. Many got free land through the federal government's Homestead Act, which granted 160 acres (65 ha) to any farmer willing to work the land for at least five years. Married couples received 320 acres (129 ha). Other new farmers bought land from railroads at relatively cheap prices. While most homesteaders were American born, many came from Germany or Scandinavian countries. New farming towns such as Gildford, Bloomfield, Shelby, Chester, Geraldine, and Joliet grew along the railroad tracks.

Montana residents claimed 32 million acres (about 13 million ha) of land under the Homestead Act, more than in any other state.

Workers building the tunnel for the Fort Peck Dam, 1930s

ALONE ON THE PLAINS

Farms in eastern Montana were isolated. The farms stood miles from each other, and farming towns were few and far between. Novelist Wallace Stegner grew up on a Montana farm. In 1955, he wrote, "We saw few people. Occasionally a Swede or Norwegian stopped by. Once in a while we drove over to see a neighbor. Once or twice a summer we went to town for supplies. A visit or a visitor was excitement, a trip to town delirium, but excitement was rare and delirium rarer. The rest of the time we communed with the gophers, weasels, badgers [and] meadow larks. . . ."

In the early 1900s, farmers were aided by ample rainfall and high wheat prices. But when these favorable conditions changed, it spelled disaster for farm families. The amount of rain that falls on the eastern plains of Montana varies greatly from year to year. In the early 1900s, the rains were adequate to grow crops. But more often, rain was scant in the east. Farmers who watered their land through irrigation survived the dry periods, but irrigation was expensive and not available to all. Also, the high prices for wheat and food products dropped in the 1920s. Many farmers in eastern Montana were forced to abandon their fields and move to what they hoped was greener land in Washington and Oregon. The 1920s has been the only decade in which Montana lost population.

DEPRESSION AND WAR

Life became even more difficult for Montanans in 1929, when the Great Depression began. This severe economic downturn affected everyone in the country. Factories closed, banks went out of business, farmers could not sell their goods. Many people had trouble putting food on the table.

The Depression hit the copper industry hard as cheap copper flooded into the country from Africa and South America. Thousands of miners lost their jobs in Butte and Anaconda. Montana farms felt the double blow of falling prices and drought.

In 1932, Americans facing the Depression elected Franklin Roosevelt president. They rallied behind his New Deal program, which aimed to provide jobs by spending money on public projects, help suffering Americans, and rescue the economy. In Montana alone, a New Deal agency called the Works Progress Administration built 7,239 miles (11,650 km) of highways, 1,366 bridges, 301 school buildings, 30 public swimming pools, and 10 ski jumps. Another New Deal organization, the Civilian Conservation Corps (CCC), provided work for young people. CCC youth built many park facilities, including the visitors' lodge at the Lewis and Clark Caverns near Three Forks. The biggest of all New Deal projects in Montana was the construction of the Fort Peck Dam along the Missouri River in northeastern Montana. In 1936, during the peak of its construction, 10,500 people worked on the Peck Dam.

The New Deal programs did not end the Great Depression, but they brought some relief. The Depression did not end until World War II began in Europe in 1939. Soon Great Britain, Russia, and other countries were trying to stop German aggression. Then

Until well into the 20th century, most Montana residents were born outside the state. In 1936, Roy E. Ayers was elected the 11th governor of Montana. He was the first native-born Montanan to serve as governor.

A bulldozer in action at the Anaconda
Copper Mining Company log camp, 1943

on December 7, 1941, Japanese planes bombed the U.S. naval base at Pearl Harbor, Hawai'i. Americans were stunned. The country immediately declared war on Japan, an ally of Germany, and American soldiers went overseas to fight in both Europe and Asia. Before the war ended, more than 1,500 Montanans had lost their lives.

World War II created a great military need for metals, coal, and other mine products. This helped bring Montana's mining industry out of its slump. The logging industry also expanded. Abundant rains in the early 1940s helped farmers, and crop prices rose because of the wartime demand. The war also caused massive shifts in the state's population. Factories in Washington and California, which produced airplanes and other war goods, offered high wages to workers. Many Montanans left to take jobs in other states. They did not return to Montana even after the war ended in 1945.

Standing Up for Her Beliefs

President Franklin Roosevelt spoke to Congress the day after the Japanese attack on Pearl Harbor amid an atmosphere of shock and outrage. He called December 7, 1941, "a date which will live in **infamy**." The president then asked Congress for a declaration of war against Japan. All congresspeople except for one voted for war. The lone dissenter was Jeannette Rankin of Montana. Her two goals in life were to achieve rights for women and to stop war. She combined the two goals, believing that women had the duty to bring peace and civility into human lives. At the time, women were not part of the regular army. "As a woman I can't go to war," Rankin said, "and I refuse to send anyone else."

Rankin voted against going to war at a time when the country's desire for revenge against Japan was at fever pitch. Was she correct in defying the mood of the people of her country and voting with her conscience?

MODERN MONTANA

Montana's economy went through sweeping changes in the years after the war. Low prices for farm goods forced more farm families to give up their land and move to cities. Copper declined as a major product in the state. The Anaconda Company switched from mining copper to aluminum. Oil was discovered in northeastern Montana, and wells began pumping in the 1950s. The mining of coal and natural gas also rose in importance.

By 1970, tourism had passed mining as the state's leading source of income. Tourism thrived as people came to enjoy themselves in Montana's magnificent parks and vast forests. Glacier National Park delighted growing numbers of out-of-state visitors. Private companies built hotels and golf courses to take advantage of Montana's spectacular vistas. Ski resorts, such as the

WORD TO KNOW

infamy *an evil reputation*

one in the town of Red Lodge, kept tourism alive in the winter months.

In 1972, Montanans wrote a new constitution, which went into effect the following year. The new constitution changed some rules regarding taxes and strengthened the legislature and the office of the governor. It also acknowledged the environmental movement, which was gaining strength across the country. The constitution guaranteed Montanans the "right to a clean and healthful environment." As part of this growing concern with keeping the land healthy, the state passed a law in 1973 requiring that land damaged by mining be restored to its natural state.

Meanwhile Montana, which is home to people mostly of European descent, was becoming more diverse. In 1974, an African American named Geraldine Travis made history when she was elected to the state legislature from a predominantly white area. Many Latinos, or people of Hispanic descent, arrived during the 1970s and 1980s, often settling in the Billings area. And Montana continued to be home to large Native American communities. Still, Montana remained among the states with the highest proportion of white residents in the country. Its overwhelmingly white population led to the charge, which most Montanans dispute, that the state was a haven for white racists.

In the 1990s, as the Internet Age began to take off, most people saw the benefits of new technologies. But a fearful handful tried to avoid the changing world by hiding in Montana's isolated mountain regions. In 1994, brothers John and David Trochmann formed the **Militia** of Montana in the town of Noxon. The militia was a **white supremacist** group that advocated establishing a separate country exclusively for white

Geraldine Travis

WORDS TO KNOW

militia *an army made up of citizens trained to serve as soldiers in an emergency*

white supremacist *one who believes in the superiority of the white race over other races*

A skier at Whitefish Mountain Resort

people in the northwestern United States. The militia attracted few followers. Two years later, law officers captured Theodore Kaczynski, who was known as the Unabomber, living in a cabin in Lincoln, Montana. Kaczynski protested technological advances and terrified Americans by sending lethal letter bombs. The Unabomber had no long-standing ties with Montana. He graduated from Harvard University and taught at the University of California at Berkeley, but he used Big Sky Country as a hiding place.

In the 21st century, tourism continued to flourish in Montana. And why not? Big Sky Country has sparkling rivers and lakes, snow-covered mountains, winter wonders, and wildlife. Everything an outdoor-loving tourist wishes for abounds in Montana.

READ ABOUT

A dancer at Milk
River Indian Days
in Fort Belknap

CHAPTER SIX

PEOPLE

★

MONTANANS HAVE A PROUD REPUTATION AS FRIENDLY PEOPLE WHO ARE QUICK TO WELCOME VISITORS AND MAKE THEM FEEL RIGHT AT HOME. Perhaps the state's history of lonesome cattle ranches and distant farms has sparked that friendly spirit. Even today in many parts of Montana, people are few and far between. As you drive Montana's country roads, you'll notice that people on foot or in cars wave at you. Be sure to wave back. It's the Montana way.

White-water rafters in the Yellowstone River just north of Gardiner

THE MONTANA FAMILY

Years ago, many people came to Montana to work in the mining and logging industries. They settled in the region and started communities and raised families. Today, the vast majority of Montana residents are of European descent. Their ancestors came from Great Britain, Scotland, Ireland, Germany, and Scandinavian countries such as Norway, Sweden, and Finland.

Some 56,000 Native Americans, about 6 percent of the state's total population, live in Montana. Most of them reside on one of the state's seven major reservations: Flathead, Fort Belknap, Blackfoot, Rocky Boy's, Fort Peck, Northern Cheyenne, and Crow. Members of 11 different nations live on these reservations.

People QuickFacts

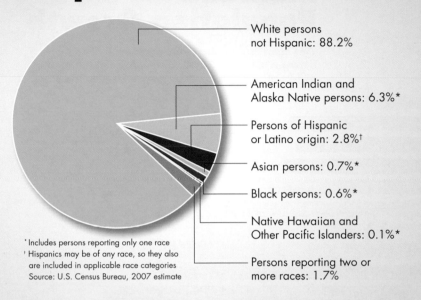

White persons
not Hispanic: 88.2%

American Indian and
Alaska Native persons: 6.3%*

Persons of Hispanic
or Latino origin: 2.8%†

Asian persons: 0.7%*

Black persons: 0.6%*

Native Hawaiian and
Other Pacific Islanders: 0.1%*

Persons reporting two or
more races: 1.7%

* Includes persons reporting only one race
† Hispanics may be of any race, so they also
 are included in applicable race categories
 Source: U.S. Census Bureau, 2007 estimate

IMPROVING HEALTH CARE

Lois Fister Steele (1939–), who belongs to the Assiniboine Nation, grew up on the Fort Peck Reservation in Poplar, Montana. In 1978, she earned a medical degree from the University of Minnesota and became a doctor. Beginning in 1986, she devoted her efforts to directing the Indians into Medicine Program at the University of North Dakota, which has helped to increase the number of Native American doctors in the United States from 16 to 60. Steele continues to work to develop a health program that is controlled and delivered by Native Americans to Native Americans.

Montana's Hispanic population grew 40 percent in the 1990s. The state's largest Hispanic community is in Billings. The state is also home to small numbers of African Americans, mostly in Great Falls, and Asian Americans.

EAST AND WEST

More than 100 years ago, during the homesteading era, Montana's leaders imagined the eastern part of the state being a land of farms and thriving farm towns. Although the plains were a good prospect, the dream faded because rainfall in eastern Montana is not consistent enough to sustain farms. In recent years, many people from eastern Montana have moved to the west, where there are more jobs in the tourism

An average of just 7 people live in every square mile (3 per sq km) of Montana. Only two other states—Alaska and Wyoming—have a lower population density.

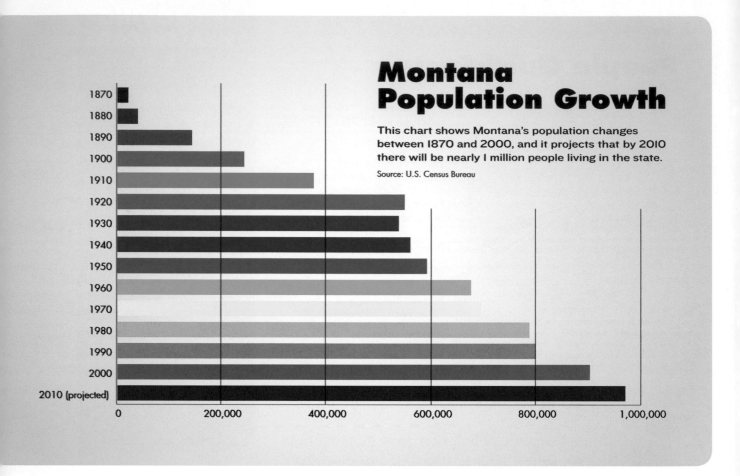

Montana Population Growth

This chart shows Montana's population changes between 1870 and 2000, and it projects that by 2010 there will be nearly 1 million people living in the state.

Source: U.S. Census Bureau

Big City Life

This list shows the population of Montana's biggest cities.

Billings 98,721
Missoula 62,923
Great Falls 56,338
Bozeman 33,535
Helena 27,383

Source: U.S. Census Bureau, 2006 estimate

industry. Today, most Montanans live in the western third of the state.

COUNTRY LIFE AND CITY LIFE

Through most of the state's history, the majority of Montanans lived in rural areas. Today, 54 percent reside in cities and towns. This makes Montana more rural than most of the nation. Across the country, 25 percent of people live in rural areas. Only three Montana cities—Billings, Missoula, and Great Falls—are large enough to be classified as a metropolitan area, a central city that supports suburbs.

Where Montanans Live

The colors on this map indicate population density throughout the state. The darker the color, the more people live there.

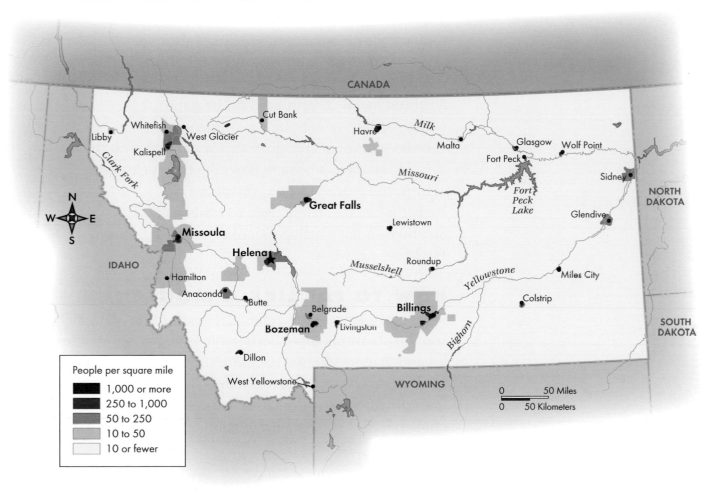

City life offers certain advantages, such as easy access to schools and hospitals. There are also more jobs for young people in cities. But traffic is worse in cities, and crime, which is infrequent everywhere in Montana, is higher in urban areas. Many Montanans grew up in wide-open spaces, and they enjoy that lifestyle and choose to remain in the country.

HOW TO TALK LIKE A MONTANAN

Here are a few words you might hear in Montana:

Barrow pit—ditch on the side of a road that helps
drain the road

Critter—cow, horse, or other range animal

Dogs—aside from domestic dogs, Montanans often call
wild coyotes "dogs"

Dryland farm—a farm with no irrigation

Gully washer—a very heavy rainstorm

Gumbo—in Louisiana, gumbo is a seafood stew, but
in Montana it is used to describe the sticky mud of
unpaved roads after a rainstorm

Potbelly—a large truck used to transport cattle

Swather—a hay-cutting machine used on farms

Waddie—a cowboy

HOW TO EAT LIKE A MONTANAN

Most early Montanans relied on bison for food. Today,
some restaurants serve buffalo burgers, but Montanans
are much more likely to eat hamburgers. Many Montana
foods take advantage of the state's natural resources by
including ingredients such as trout, huckleberries, and
chokecherries. The state's farmers' markets offer fresh
produce of all kinds.

A farmers' market in Helena

MENU

WHAT'S ON THE MENU IN MONTANA?

★ ★ ★

Pan-fried trout

Pan-fried Trout

Many people travel to Montana just to fish for trout. If they catch a trout, one of the favorite ways to cook it is to dip it in raw egg, roll it in cracker crumbs, and cook it in a frying pan over a campfire.

Venison Steaks

Deer hunting is also popular in Montana. A delicious preparation for venison (deer meat) is to cut it into steaks, marinate them in olive oil and garlic, and then broil.

Butte Pasty

Welsh miners took these hearty pastries filled with meat, potato, and vegetables with them into the mines to eat for lunch. Today, they remain popular in Butte and throughout the state.

Skillet Cookies

These cookies are made by mixing nuts, dried fruit, sugar, butter, and eggs together in a skillet. When the mixture is cooled, stir in rice cereal, roll into balls, and roll in coconut.

Huckleberry Pie

Huckleberries are similar to blueberries, and they grow wild in parts of Montana. Fill a pie with them, and you'll have a mouthwatering dessert.

TRY THIS RECIPE
Indian Fry Bread

Here is a simple recipe for a traditional Native American dish. In good times, fry bread was accompanied by meat and potatoes; in bad times, it was the entire meal. This recipe comes from Earl Old Person, a former leader of the Blackfoot Nation of Montana. Be sure to have an adult nearby to help

Ingredients:
6 cups flour
3 tablespoons baking powder
1½ teaspoons salt
2½ cups water

Instructions:
1. Stir the flour, baking powder, and salt together in a bowl.
2. Slowly add the water and knead (work with the fingers) until the dough is soft but not sticky. Add more water if necessary.
3. Grease a 9" x 9" baking pan and spread the dough inside.
4. Bake at 350°F for 35 minutes. Eat the fry bread hot with a dash of butter or jelly.

Huckleberry pie

Students work with molten glass during an art class at Box Elder School.

SCHOOLS

Some of Montana's first schools were established in mining camps in the 1860s. The camp schools were private, and the students—many of whom were adults who wanted to learn to read—paid to attend.

Today, Montana's public school system is run by an elected official called the superintendent of public instruction and 11 members of the Board of Public Education, who are appointed by the governor. Montana students are high achievers. In 2007, Montana eighth graders ranked third among the 50 states in reading and tenth in math.

Montana's largest colleges are Montana State University in Bozeman and the University of Montana in Missoula. Montana Tech, in Butte, is devoted specifically to mine engineering. Montana also has four tribal colleges that serve Native Americans on reservations, including Salish Kootenai College and Little Big Horn College.

ARTISTS

Montana's natural environment has moved artists to paint, sculpt, write, and photograph. Bob Stayton of Bigfork is a sculptor and story-teller whose bronze statues expertly capture Montana wildlife such as deer on the run. Some of the stories Stayton tells come from tales told to him by his Native American ances-tors. Michael Meissner of Glendive, who paints wildlife scenes, can trace his family roots in Montana to the 1840s. Amber Jean, a wild-life artist who lives in Livingston, needs to be close to nature to do

Wildlife artist Amber Jean (left) sits with fellow artist Tony Alvis on her bison-themed bench. The sculpture was carved in wood, then cast in bronze.

MINI-BIO

CHARLES M. RUSSELL: WESTERN ARTIST

Charles Marion Russell (1864–1926) was one of the great artists of the American West. His paintings and sculptures bring to life the people, animals, and landscapes he found there. Russell was born in Missouri and settled in Great Falls as a young man. He worked as a cowboy and taught himself to paint. For years, he was unable to make a living as an artist, and he sometimes gave his paintings to tavern owners in exchange for food and drink. The owners got a bargain. In 2005, a Russell paint-ing sold at auction for $5.6 million.

? Want to know more? See www. sidrichardsonmuseum.org/cmr.html

SEE IT HERE!

A LIVELY MUSEUM

The Museum of the Plains Indian, which stands in Browning, displays Native American arts and crafts. Every July, Native Americans from the region and from Canada gather on the museum grounds for four days of art exhibits, dancing, feasting, and fun.

Musicians at the Montana Fiddlers Picnic in Livingston

her work. She spends winters in a Montana mountain cabin with no electricity or running water. One of Montana's most successful artists, Charles M. Russell, made a name for himself painting cowboys, Native Americans, and western landscapes.

MUSICAL MONTANA

People have been making music in Montana for thousands of years. Songs and dances were and are important in Native American cultures. Cowboys sang songs to pass the lonely hours on the range. Today, country music is popular throughout the state. Students of classical music attend the Montana Chamber Music Workshop at Montana State University. The Bozeman Symphony, a classical music orchestra, celebrated its 40th birthday in the 2007–08 concert season.

Fantasy novel writer Christopher Paolini is from Paradise Valley.

WRITERS

Many Montanans have used their home state in their writing. Dorothy Marie Johnson was born in Iowa in the early 20th century and moved to Montana with her family when she was young. In Whitefish, she wrote short stories and novels, most of them about pioneers and the American West. Three of her stories, including "The Man Who Shot Liberty Valance," became Hollywood movies.

Ivan Doig, who grew up in a family of homesteaders and sheepherders in White Sulphur Springs, has written many novels based on his youth in rural Montana. His book *This House of Sky: Landscapes of a Western Mind* was nominated for the National Book Award in 1979.

Christopher Paolini has been inspired by the beauty of his home in Montana's Paradise Valley, but he writes about a very different world. Paolini, who was born in 1983, is the author of fantasy novels such as *Eragon*, which is set in the mystical kingdom of Alagaësia. He wrote the book when he was a teenager!

MINI-BIO

SNEED COLLARD III: CHILDREN'S AUTHOR

Sneed Collard III is a children's book author who lives in Missoula. He has published more than 50 books. Collard has written popular middle-grade novels such as *Dog Sense* and *Double Eagle*. He is also well known for his science books. In 2006, he received the Washington Post–Children's Book Guild Nonfiction Award for books such as *The Prairie Builders*. "There is a huge gap between what scientists know and what [other] humans know," he says. "One of the reasons I wanted to be a writer is to close that gap."

🌙 **Want to know more?** See www.sneedbcollardiii.com

NAME CHANGE

Joe Montana (who has no relation to the state) was a great pro football quarterback in the 1980s and 1990s. In 1993, the town of Ismay in southeastern Montana, which had a population of only 20, temporarily changed its name to Joe. It was a publicity stunt designed to get Joe Montana to come to his namesake town. It didn't work. Joe Montana never visited Joe, Montana.

Wallace Stegner grew up in Great Falls. He wrote more than a dozen novels, many about the western experience. Stegner was a versatile author, and his themes and settings changed often. His novel *The Spectator Bird,* which takes place in Denmark after World War II, won the 1977 National Book Award.

A. B. Guthrie Jr., who lived in Choteau, wrote many books on the American West, including *The Way West,* which won the Pulitzer Prize for Fiction in 1950, and *The Big Sky.* Montana took the nickname "Big Sky Country" from this book.

Few other writers express the love and admiration of Montana more elegantly than K. Ross Toole. Born in Missoula in 1920 to a long-standing Montana family, Toole eventually became the director of the Montana Historical Society. In his writings, he praised his state's efforts to preserve its environment. His history *Montana: An Uncommon Land* is a testament to the state he loved.

OUTDOOR FUN

Rodeo has been popular in Montana for more than 100 years, since the days when cowboys rode the range. More than 25 rodeos are held in the state annually. The oldest, the Wild Horse Stampede, is held in Wolf Point. The Crow Fair is a Native American rodeo that attracts more than 40,000 people each year. The town of Three Forks holds a rodeo restricted to high school students who dream of becoming rodeo stars.

A matchup between the Helena Senators and the Billings Royals in 2002

There are no major league professional teams in Montana, but Billings, Butte, and Missoula boast minor league baseball teams. Football and basketball fans cheer for the University of Montana Grizzlies and the Montana State University Bobcats. The Grizzlies and the Bobcats football teams first played each other in 1897, and the rivalry between the two schools is legendary.

Activities in the great outdoors are by far the favorite sports in Montana. The state has 14,633 miles (23,550 km) of marked hiking trails. Only California has more hiking trails than Montana. With 1,900 lakes and 21,000 miles (34,000 km) of rivers, Montana is a paradise for fishers. Winter is a busy season, too, because Montana has 14,000 acres (5,670 ha) of ski areas and 548 downhill runs. Snowmobile fans claim Montana has the greatest snowmobile paths in the nation.

The town of Ennis in southwestern Montana has a sign claiming it is home to "660 people and 11 million trout."

READ ABOUT

Students and legislators watch as Governor Brian Schweitzer signs a no-smoking bill in 2005.

CHAPTER SEVEN

GOVERNMENT

★

IN ITS WILD WEST PAST, MONTANA WAS CONDEMNED AS A LAWLESS AND DANGEROUS PLACE. Back then, gold seekers and cowboys sometimes got into deadly gunfights. Today, with its very low crime rate, Montana is one of the safest states in the nation. Government and the rule of law have helped bring order to Montana.

The state capitol in Helena

KIDS AND STATE SYMBOLS

Students cannot vote until they are 18, but they do have a voice in Montana's state government before that. Kids help choose the state symbols such as the state bird and the state fossil. This practice of allowing children to select state symbols has a long history in Montana. In 1930, schoolchildren throughout the state held an election and chose the Western meadowlark as the official state bird.

Schoolkids were given the task of choosing the state animal in 1982, and that election aroused many arguments. Some 55,000 students in 425 schools debated which animal should represent Montana. The final two contestants were the grizzly bear and the elk. One pro-grizzly student wrote, "By its very size, strength, and beauty the grizzly represents an awesome spectacle. Montana has the same characteristics." An anti-grizzly voter pointed out, "The grizzly by its very nature is not a friendly animal. Montanans, on the other hand, are friendly." In the end, the grizzly defeated the elk to become the state animal.

THE CONSTITUTION

Montana's current constitution became law in 1973. It replaced the state's original constitution, which had been written in 1889. Amendments (changes) to the constitution must be approved by voters in a regular election. Montana's constitution divides state government into three branches: executive, legislative, and judicial.

Capitol Facts

Here are some fascinating facts about Montana's state capitol.

- Construction of the capitol began in 1889 and was completed, as planned, on July 4, 1902.
- In 1912, two wings were added to the building.
- The building's dome is made from Anaconda copper.
- The dome rises 165 feet (50 m) above the ground.
- On top of the dome stands a statue called the Goddess of Liberty.
- Inside hangs a huge painting, *Lewis and Clark Meeting the Flatheads in Ross's Hole*, by Montana artist Charles M. Russell. This painting is 25 feet (7.6 m) long and 12 feet (3.7 m) high. It re-creates the meeting between explorers Lewis and Clark and the Salish people of Montana.

Capital City

This map shows places of interest in Helena, Montana's capital city.

- Holter Museum of Art
- Original Governor's Mansion
- Montana Historical Society
- Ghost Art Gallery
- **HELENA**
- Montana Heritage Commission
- Montana State Capitol

SEE IT HERE!

MONTANA'S ORIGINAL GOVERNOR'S MANSION

One of the handsomest buildings in Montana served as a governor's mansion for almost 50 years. In 1888, a wealthy investor named William Chessman built a lavish home in Helena for his family. The brick mansion stayed in private hands until 1913, when the state bought it for use as the governor's mansion. The mansion is no longer used as the governor's home, but the Montana Historical Society has lovingly restored the building.

EXECUTIVE BRANCH

The executive branch is headed by the governor and the lieutenant governor, both of whom are elected to four-year terms. The governor appoints many state officials. He or she also submits a budget to the legislature and recommends laws and programs. The constitution grants the governor broad powers, including the right to call out the state militia in cases of emergency. The lieutenant governor takes over if the governor is unable to serve. In 2000, Judy Martz was elected the state's first female governor.

Other major officials in the executive branch are the attorney general, who is the leading lawyer for the state; the auditor, who keeps track of the state's finances; the secretary of state, who oversees elections; and the superintendent of public instruction, who is in charge of schools.

LEGISLATIVE BRANCH

Montana's legislative branch is made up of two parts: a 50-member senate and a 100-member house of representatives. Senators are elected to four-year terms; members of the house serve two-year terms.

Members of both legislative bodies meet in the state capitol to discuss proposed laws, called bills. When senators and house members agree on the details of a bill, it is sent to the governor for his or her signature. If the governor signs the bill, it becomes law. The gover-

---

MINI-BIO

ELLA KNOWLES: GROUNDBREAKING LAWYER

Ella Knowles (1860–1911) was the first woman licensed to practice law in Montana. In 1892, she became the first woman to run for the office of attorney general. She lost the election by a narrow margin and later married the man who defeated her, Henri Haskell. Knowles became a successful attorney and argued cases before the United States Supreme Court.

 Want to know more? See http://montanakids.com/cool_stories/Famous_Montanans/haskell.htm

An assistant district attorney presents a case to the Montana Supreme Court in 2001.

nor can also veto, or reject, the bill. If two-thirds of the members of each house vote again for the bill, they can override the veto.

JUDICIAL BRANCH

The highest court in Montana is the state supreme court. The seven members of this court review decisions made in district courts, which are the state's major trial courts. Municipal, city, and other courts hear less-serious cases.

MIKE MANSFIELD: POWERFUL POLITICAL LEADER

Mike Mansfield (1903–2001) was born in New York City and as a boy moved with his family to Great Falls. In 1917, at age 14, he lied about his age and joined the U.S. Navy to serve in World War I. When he returned home, he worked as a miner and attended the University of Montana. He became a history professor and then a member of Congress. He won a seat in the U.S. Senate in 1952 and served as Senate majority leader from 1961 to 1977, the longest such term ever in the Senate. Mansfield disapproved of U.S. involvement in Vietnam and was one of the nation's leading critics of the Vietnam War. Mansfield became ambassador to Japan after he retired from the Senate in 1977.

 Want to know more? See www.senate.gov/artandhistory/history/common/generic/People_Leaders_Mansfield.htm

WEIRD AND WACKY LAWS

Most of the time, lawmakers in Montana write laws that are sensible and helpful to the state. But in the past the legislature created some laws that are strange by today's standards. Do you think these are still enforced?

- It is illegal for a woman to open her husband's mail.
- A driver cannot have a sheep in the cab of his or her truck.
- A married woman cannot go fishing alone on Sundays, and unmarried women cannot fish alone at all.
- In Billings, it is illegal to keep a rat as a pet.

Montana State Government

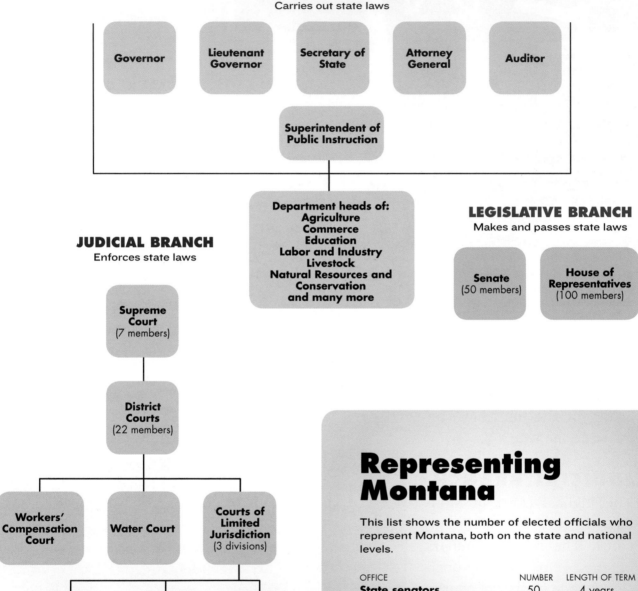

EXECUTIVE BRANCH
Carries out state laws

Governor

Lieutenant Governor

Secretary of State

Attorney General

Auditor

Superintendent of Public Instruction

Department heads of:
Agriculture
Commerce
Education
Labor and Industry
Livestock
Natural Resources and Conservation
and many more

LEGISLATIVE BRANCH
Makes and passes state laws

Senate
(50 members)

House of Representatives
(100 members)

JUDICIAL BRANCH
Enforces state laws

Supreme Court
(7 members)

District Courts
(22 members)

Workers' Compensation Court

Water Court

Courts of Limited Jurisdiction
(3 divisions)

Justice Courts
(66 members)

Municipal Courts
(5 members)

City Courts
(81 members)

Representing Montana

This list shows the number of elected officials who represent Montana, both on the state and national levels.

OFFICE	NUMBER	LENGTH OF TERM
State senators	50	4 years
State representatives	100	2 years
U.S. senators	2	6 years
U.S. representatives	1	2 years
Presidential electors	3	—

LOCAL GOVERNMENT

Montana has 56 counties. Most counties are governed by three county commissioners, each elected to a six-year term. Mayors and city councils generally rule cities. Local governments are responsible for maintaining roads and providing police and fire protection.

Montana Counties

This map shows the 56 counties in Montana. Helena, the state capital, is indicated with a star.

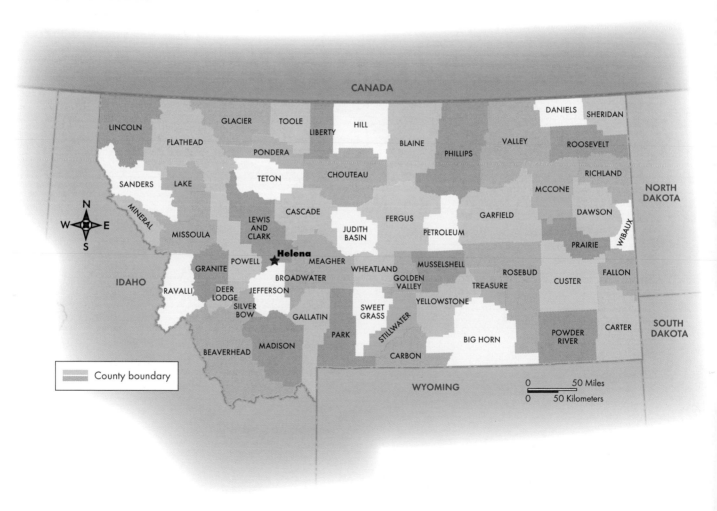

State Flag

Montana's state flag was adapted from a banner carried by the first Montana volunteers in 1898, during the Spanish-American War. The flag is a deep blue color, with the state seal at the center. The flag was adopted in 1905.

State Seal

A plow and a miner's pick and shovel sit at the center of the state seal, representing important resources in the state. The right side of the seal features the Great Falls of the Missouri River, and the left side shows the Rocky Mountains. Near the bottom are the Spanish words *Oro y Plata*, which mean "gold and silver."

The seal was first adopted when Montana was a territory. Francis McGee Thompson, a representative in the First Legislative Assembly, submitted the original design, and the seal was approved on February 9, 1865. The seal was again approved when Montana became a state in 1889.

An instructor points out deer tracks at Glacier National Park.

CHAPTER EIGHT

ECONOMY

★

MONTANA'S ECONOMY FIRST BOOMED WHEN GOLD WAS DISCOVERED THERE IN THE 1860s. Later, people came to the region in search of silver or copper, or to raise cattle or wheat. Today, tourism is the single most important source of jobs and income within the state.

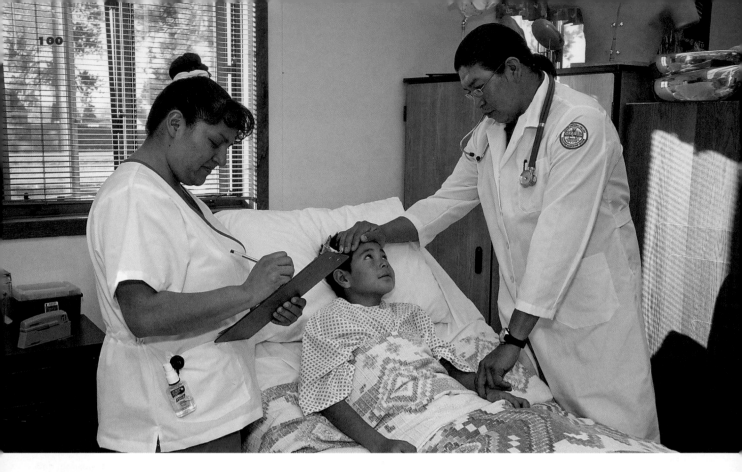

Montana's doctors and nurses are service workers who help care for the people of the state.

FAQ ★★★

Q: **WHO IS MONTANA'S SINGLE LARGEST EMPLOYER?**

A: The government. State, city, and federal government employees make up 21 percent of the workforce in Montana.

SERVICE JOBS

Every year, thousands of young Montanans graduate from school and look for jobs. Where is the best place to find work? Most Montanans—about 80 percent of the workforce—are service workers. A service worker is not involved in making a product such as pickup trucks or raising cattle on a ranch or digging copper from the earth. Instead, service workers provide services that customers are willing to pay for. A doctor is a service worker, as are teachers, police officers, and store clerks. Tourism is a leading source of jobs in the state. Most people involved in the tourist industry, such as restaurant and hotel staff, are service workers.

Over the years, the falling price of metals, particularly copper, hurt Montana's employment rate. With the rise of tourism, however, the picture brightened.

What Do Montanans Do?

This color-coded chart shows what industries Montanans work in.

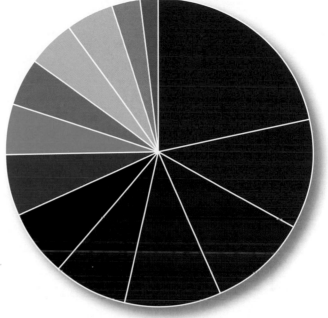

21.7%	Educational services, health care, and social assistance, 101,347
11.6%	Retail trade, 54,196
10.3%	Arts, entertainment, recreation, accommodation, and food services, 48,112
10.1%	Construction, 47,352

7.7%	Agriculture, forestry, fishing, hunting, and mining, 36,061
7.1%	Professional, scientific, management, administrative, and waste management services, 33,365
6.3%	Public administration, 29,275
5.3%	Finance, insurance, real estate, rental, and leasing, 24,647

5.1%	Other services, except public administration, 24,016
5.0%	Manufacturing, 23,192
4.9%	Transportation, warehousing, and utilities, 22,656
3.0%	Wholesale trade, 14,195
1.9%	Information, 9,061

Source: U.S. Census Bureau, 2006 estimate

FROM THE FARM

Farmland covers almost two-thirds of Montana. Wheat is the state's largest single crop. Year after year, Montana ranks high among the nation's top wheat-producing states. Montana farmers also grow barley, hay, dry beans, potatoes, and sugar beets.

Montana is one of the nation's leading livestock producers and has some of the nation's largest ranches. Ranchers raise dairy cows, beef cattle, sheep, hogs, and horses. Beef cattle and sheep are found throughout the state. The most productive dairy regions are in the river

Ranchers on horseback round up cattle in the foothills of the Crazy Mountains.

The small town of Two Dot, along the Musselshell River, was named after cattleman H. J. "Two Dot" Wilson, who branded his cattle with two dots.

valleys of western Montana. Pickup trucks and tractors perform heavy work on the ranches, but many ranchers also use horses. The cowboy era and respect for horses remain alive in Montana.

MADE IN MONTANA

Only about 5 percent of the Montana workforce holds manufacturing jobs. Most of Montana's manufacturing companies turn raw materials into finished products. Oil is a leading product, and there are major oil-refining operations in Billings and Great Falls. Sawmills in western Montana turn trees into plywood and other building materials. Trees are also turned into telephone poles.

Food processing is important in Montana as well. Some plants buy milk from dairy farms and process it into cheese. Other factories mill raw wheat into flour.

Major Agricultural and Mining Products

This map shows where Montana's major agricultural and mining products come from. See a cow? That means cattle are raised there.

Cattle	Lead
Coal	Mineral mining
Copper	Natural gas
Dairy	Oil
Forest products	Potatoes
Fruit	Sheep
Gold	Silver
Grains	Sugar beets
Hay	

- Urban area
- Forests, some farming
- Grazing, rangeland
- Farming

A worker at a Montana copper smelter, where metal is processed

The Stillwater Mine near Nye, Montana, is the only platinum mine in North America.

SEE IT HERE!

VIRGINIA CITY

Virginia City, once a mining boomtown, is today an open-air museum that preserves Montana's wild and rugged gold-mining frontier. The town reached its glory days in the 1870s, but when the gold ran out it almost became a ghost town. Today, Virginia City is a tourist center. A major attraction is the Alder Gulch monument, which commemorates the spot where gold was discovered in 1863.

MINING

Mining was Montana's first boom industry. Some people became rich mining the gold and silver found below the earth's surface. The state's copper mines later contributed even more wealth to the state.

Today, mining products are less important to the state's economy than they were in the past. Many foreign nations produce cheap copper, and Montana struggles to compete with them. Also, mining has become automated, and machines now do the work that huge crews of miners used to perform.

DIGGINGS IN HELENA

Dig a basement for a new house in Helena and you might attract a crowd of onlookers. To this day, traces of gold and silver can be found below the city's surface.

Montana mines still turn out copper, gold, silver, and lead. Montana's Beartooth Mountains also produce platinum, a metal even more valuable than gold. Most mines that yield metal ores are in the Rocky Mountain region.

Oil and natural gas are found in eastern Montana. Montana ranks tenth among the states in oil production. Montana is also rich in coal. The coal mines are found in the southeastern part of the state.

Talc, which is used to make talcum powder, is mined in Montana. Sand, gravel, and limestone are also mined in the state. The single most exotic product of the state's mines is the Yogo sapphire, a magnificent blue gemstone found only in Montana.

This worker checks on an oil pump in Whitlash.

Top Products

Agriculture Wheat, barley, dairy cattle, beef cattle, wool, flaxseed, honey, lentils, peas

Manufacturing Refined oil, wood products, food processing

Mining Coal, oil, natural gas, copper, gold, silver, lead, platinum

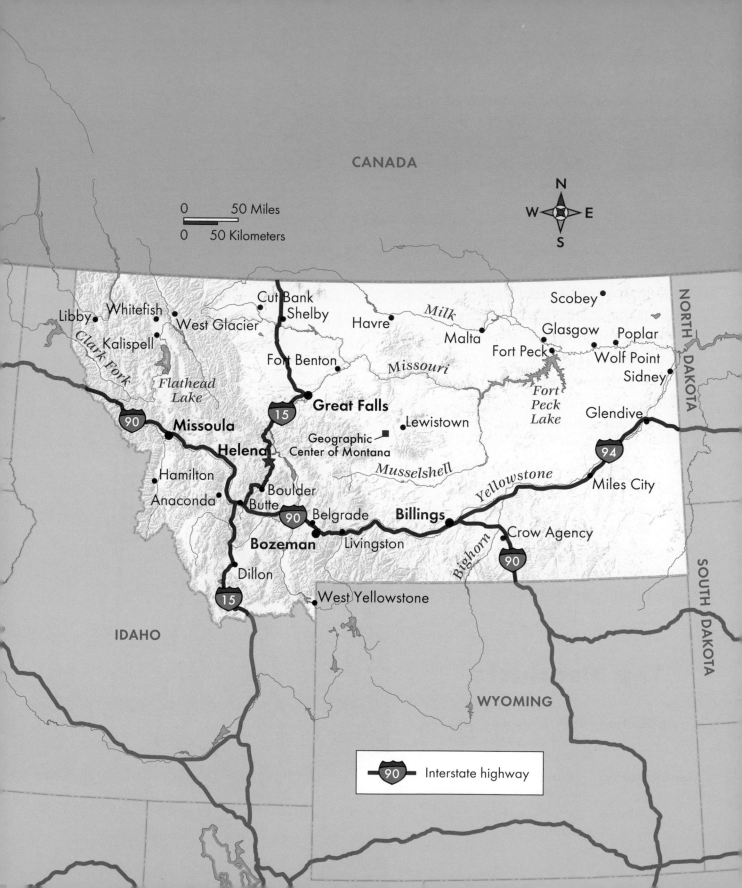

CHAPTER NINE

TRAVEL GUIDE

TRAVEL GUIDE

★

MONTANA IS NICKNAMED THE TREASURE STATE, AND IT IS A TREASURE FOR VISITORS. The state is chock-full of awesome scenery, exciting Wild West history, and interesting towns. Montana has so many things to do and see that some people devote a lifetime to exploring the region. We'll begin our tour now, so grab your map and let's get going!

← Follow along with this travel map. We'll begin in Libby and end our trip in Wolf Point.

THE NORTHWEST

THINGS TO DO: Hike through towering trees, race down the slopes at Big Mountain, and enjoy the jaw-dropping views along Going-to-the-Sun Road.

Libby

★ **Libby Creek Gold Panning Area:** In the 1800s, gold mines operated in Libby. Today, visitors are encouraged to pan for gold—yes, specks can still be found—at Libby Creek.

★ **Kootenai National Forest:** The Kootenai National Forest covers remote northwestern Montana and spills into Idaho, comprising 2.2 million acres (900,000 ha) of tall trees. More than 20 hiking trails lead visitors over mountain ridges and along the banks of the Kootenai River. Don't miss the Kootenai Falls, a waterfall that spills over a cliff the height of an eight-story building.

A kayaker at Kootenai Falls

Whitefish Mountain Resort

Whitefish

★ **Whitefish Mountain Resort:** Thousands of skiers flock to this resort to hit the slopes of Big Mountain.

Kalispell

★ **Woodland Park:** This fine city park has a stunning rose garden.

★ **Hockaday Museum of Art:** Here you can admire fine examples of Western arts and crafts.

★ **Central School Museum:** Housed in an old school building, this museum tells the history of the National Forest Service in Montana.

West Glacier

★ **Glacier National Park:** Thousands of years ago, glaciers crawled over northern Montana and carved out a fantastic array of mountains, hills, and lakes. The Blackfoot people once called the mountains and glaciers of this region the Backbone of the World. In 1910, Glacier National Park was created. Today, the park sprawls over 1,500 square miles (3,885 sq km). Scattered throughout the park are pristine forests, alpine meadows, rugged mountains, spectacular lakes, and more than 200 waterfalls. Wildlife includes wolves, bears, bald eagles, moose, and herds of elk. Almost 2 million people a year visit the park and leave awestruck by its beauty.

Glacier National Park

SEE IT HERE!

GOING-TO-THE-SUN ROAD

Often called Sun Road, this scenic highway was completed in 1932. It runs 53 miles (85 km) across Glacier National Park. Along Sun Road is Lake McDonald, home to black bears, grizzly bears, and moose. Continue along the road and you'll pass Bird Woman Falls, a 492-foot (150 m) waterfall. Stop at Trail of the Cedars, a hiking path that weaves through groves of mighty cedar trees. Another great stop is the Weeping Wall, a series of waterfalls running down a cliff, which makes the cliff face look as if it is crying.

MELTING GLACIERS

People who are familiar with Glacier National Park have seen startling changes caused by **global warming**. There are about 50 glaciers in the park. All are shrinking, melting away because of Earth's warmer temperatures. Some experts predict that by the year 2030, the park's glaciers will have vanished. But this isn't happening only in Montana. Glaciers all over the world are shrinking.

WORD TO KNOW

global warming *an increase in temperatures around the globe, particularly as a result of pollution*

THE SOUTHWEST

THINGS TO DO: Ride an antique carousel, get a good look at a steam engine, and watch a geyser spout hot water into the sky.

Missoula

★ **The Historical Museum at Fort Missoula:** This museum is dedicated to the history of Missoula County. Today, 13 structures remain, including a lookout tower and a schoolhouse.

★ **Carousel for Missoula:** Here children are invited to ride hand-carved horses on an antique carousel.

SEE IT HERE!

BITTERROOT VALLEY

According to the Salish people, hundreds of years ago a Salish Indian woman cried because she and her children were starving in the valley of the Bitterroot River. The god of the sun heard her sobs and magically converted her tears into bitterroot plants. The root of the plant, as the name implies, was bitter. But the Salish people learned that when picked at the right time of year and properly boiled, the root was both tasty and nutritious. The bitterroot is now the state flower of Montana, and the Bitterroot Valley, which stretches out south of Missoula, is stunningly beautiful.

Yellowstone National Park

West Yellowstone

★ **Yellowstone National Park:** Established in 1872, Yellowstone is the world's first national park. Most of Yellowstone lies in Wyoming, but the park spills into Montana. The park sits atop a vast active volcano, which heats water underground. Each year, 3 million visitors flock to the park to see its spectacular spouting geysers and boiling mud pots.

Butte

★ **The World Museum of Mining:** Visitors to this museum can get a good look at mining tools, a steam engine, and samples of ores.

Anaconda

★ **City Hall:** Built in 1895, the Anaconda City Hall now serves as a historical museum and arts center. Stop in and get a map telling the histories of the downtown buildings.

CENTRAL MONTANA

THINGS TO DO: Uncover frozen ancient grasshoppers, walk the streets of a ghost town, and enjoy a hair-raising drive.

Helena

★ **Montana Historical Society:** This outstanding museum presents the state's history from the time of its earliest inhabitants to the present. You can see everything from ancient Native tools to a typical kitchen from the mid-20th century.

Great Falls

★ **C. M. Russell Museum:** This museum displays sculptures and paintings of cowboys, animals, and the Western landscape by this great Montana artist and others.

★ **The Children's Museum of Montana:** At this hands-on museum, kids can dig, climb, and explore.

Lewis and Clark National Historic Trail Interpretive Center

★ **Lewis and Clark National Historic Trail Interpretive Center:** In 1805, Lewis and Clark spent a month at Great Falls, carrying their boats and supplies around the mighty waterfalls. Today, the Lewis and Clark National Historic Trail Interpretive Center brings the Lewis and Clark expedition to life with displays about their journey, the boats they used, and the tents they slept in.

The original name of Montana's capital city was **Last Chance Gulch.** In 1864, four miners stopped to pan for gold on a small creek. It was their last chance to discover gold before returning to Virginia City. They found gold, and soon other prospectors were pouring in.

Boulder

★ **Elkhorn:** This is one of Montana's best-preserved ghost towns. In the 1880s and 1890s, it had as many as 2,500 residents, and millions of dollars in gold and silver were taken from its mines. Most of the citizens left in the early 1900s, and only the ghosts remain to tell Elkhorn's story.

SEE IT HERE!

BEARTOOTH HIGHWAY

The Beartooth Highway was completed in 1936 south of Billings and is today recognized as a National Scenic Byway. The road begins at the town of Red Lodge (so named because the Crow Indians who lived there once painted their homes red) and runs 68 miles (109 km) to the Wyoming border. The road twists and turns over mountain peaks, giving travelers spectacular views. During the winter months, the Beartooth Highway is closed because it is covered with snow.

Moss Mansion

Billings

★ **Moss Mansion:** This turn-of-the-century mansion stands as a symbol of Billings's early wealthy residents.

★ **Western Heritage Center:** This art museum is housed in a stately old building that was donated to the city by Frederick Billings Jr.

★ **Rimrocks:** Visitors get a fine view of Montana's biggest city from this cliffside trail on the northern edge of town.

SEE IT HERE!

GRASSHOPPER GLACIER

About 70 miles (113 km) southwest of Billings stands Grasshopper Glacier. Hundreds of years ago, a swarm of grasshoppers, numbering in the tens of millions, was trapped here by a sudden cold snap. The insects froze and were entombed in a layer of ice. Until recent years, visitors could dig into the ice and find perfectly preserved grasshoppers. The frozen creatures can still be seen, but in fewer numbers than years past. Warmer temperatures have melted the top layer of ice and caused many of the insects to deteriorate.

THE SOUTHEAST

THINGS TO DO: Dance at the Crow Fair, look for moose and elk at Custer National Forest, and watch cowboys take on bulls at a rodeo.

Crow Agency

★ **Crow Reservation:** This reservation spreads over 37,000 square miles (96,000 sq km) and is home to about 9,300 people. The Crow people call themselves Apsaalooka, meaning "children of the large-beaked bird." Other Native people

Q: IS IT POSSIBLE TO VISIT AN INDIAN RESERVATION?

A: Absolutely! Reservations welcome visitors every day except for a few days each year during important religious occasions.

sometimes called them the "sharp people" because they were such skilled traders. On the reservation, people farm and maintain a herd of about 300 bison. Every August, the Crow Reservation hosts the Crow Fair, a grand festival. At the Crow Fair, people set up tipis, wear traditional costumes, and take part in dances.

The Crow Fair on the Crow Reservation

Miles City

★ **Range Riders Museum:** This museum brings to life the days when cattle was king in Montana. It also includes displays of Native American art and antique firearms.

★ **Miles City Bucking Horse Sale:** This citywide party combines a rodeo with an animal auction. Cowboys ride bucking broncos and bulls before the animals are offered for sale.

★ **Custer National Forest:** This national forest sprawls over three states—Montana, North Dakota, and South Dakota. In Montana, the Powder River flows through the heart of the Custer National Forest. Early soldiers noted that the Powder was "a mile wide, an inch deep."

Custer National Forest

Hiking trails wind through the Custer National Forest, and wildlife can be seen everywhere. The forest is home to moose, elk, bears, white-tailed deer, and mule deer.

★ **The Powder River Historical Museum:** This museum traces the history of the region.

THE NORTHEAST

THINGS TO DO: See the inner workings of a dam, get a close-up look at intricate Native American beadwork, and imagine you are a homesteader.

SEE IT HERE!

FORT PECK DAM

The Great Depression of the 1930s was a tragic time for people across the country and the world. Many men and women were jobless, and many families went hungry. In 1933, the U.S. government started building the Fort Peck Dam to help the people of Montana by giving them jobs. It became one of the biggest construction projects in the nation. At one point, more than 10,000 people were working on the dam. Besides creating jobs, the dam also changed northeastern Montana. The dam generated electricity, controlled flooding, and created the huge Fort Peck Lake. You can study the workings of this dam at the Fort Peck Interpretive Center and Museum.

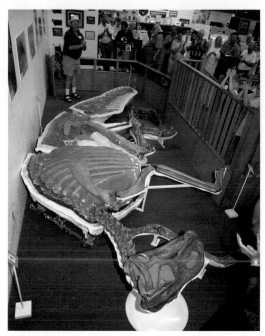

Phillips County Museum

Malta

★ **Phillips County Museum:** This museum has displays on everything from dinosaurs and outlaws to Native American beadwork and homesteaders.

Scobey

★ **Pioneer Town:** At this museum, 40 buildings re-create the atmosphere of the homesteading era.

Glasgow

★ **Charles M. Russell National Wildlife Refuge:** Deer, elk, and bighorn sheep make their home in this refuge, which lies south of the Missouri River.

★ **Valley County Pioneer Museum:** This museum tells local history through its displays about the Assiniboine people, the construction of the railroad, and the building of the Fort Peck Dam.

Poplar

★ **Poplar Museum:** The history of the Fort Peck Indian Reservation, the second-largest reservation in Montana, is the theme of this museum. Home to 10,000 Assiniboine and Sioux people, the reservation has its own post office and police department. It is served by five school districts and the Fort Peck Community College.

Wolf Point

★ **John Deere Tractor Museum:** You can see some 500 tractors, both old and new, at this museum.

John Deere tractor

WRITING PROJECTS

Check out these ideas for creating a campaign brochure and writing you-are-there narratives. Or research the lives of famous people from Montana.

118

ART PROJECTS

You can illustrate the state song, create a dazzling PowerPoint presentation, or learn about the state quarter and design your own.

119

TIMELINE

What happened when? This timeline highlights important events in the state's history—and shows what was happening throughout the United States at the same time.

122

FAST FACTS

Use this section to find fascinating facts about state symbols, land area and population statistics, weather, sports teams, and much more.

126

GLOSSARY

Remember the Words to Know from the chapters in this book? They're all collected here.

125

SCIENCE, TECHNOLOGY, & MATH PROJECTS

Make weather maps, graph population statistics, and research endangered species that live in the state.

120

PRIMARY VS. SECONDARY SOURCES

121

So what are primary and secondary sources? And what's the diff? This section explains all that and where you can find them.

BIOGRAPHICAL DICTIONARY

133

This at-a-glance guide highlights some of the state's most important and influential people. Visit this section and read about their contributions to the state, the country, and the world.

RESOURCES

Books, Web sites, DVDs, and more. Take a look at these additional sources for information about the state.

137

WRITING PROJECTS

★ ★ ★

Write a Memoir, Journal, or Editorial for Your School Newspaper!

Picture Yourself . . .

★ As a Blackfoot bison hunter on the Great Plains. Your people depend on you for food, so you are determined to succeed. Explain different ways you can hunt bison. Also describe how hunting bison changes after you acquire a horse. What is it like to hunt on horseback?

SEE: Chapter Two, page 29.

GO TO: http://montanakids.com/history_and_prehistory/buffalo_jumps/pishkuns.htm

★ Searching for gold in Montana. Write journal entries describing your trip to Montana. Then write about the other prospectors you meet. Do they seem trustworthy, or do you worry that they might steal from you? Describe how you pan for gold. What hardships and frustrations do you endure?

SEE: Chapters Three and Four, pages 41, 43–47.

GO TO: http://montanakids.com/cool_stories/ghost_towns/mining.htm

Create an Election Brochure or Web Site!

Run for office! Throughout this book, you've read about some of the issues that concern Montana today. As a candidate for governor of Montana, create a campaign brochure or Web site.

★ Explain how you meet the qualifications to be governor of Montana.

★ Talk about the three or four major issues you'll focus on if you're elected.

★ Remember, you'll be responsible for Montana's budget. How would you spend the taxpayers' money?

SEE: Chapter Seven, page 92.

GO TO: Montana's government Web site at www.mt.gov. You should also read some local newspapers. Try these:

Billings Gazette at www.billingsgazette.com

Great Falls Tribune at www.greatfallstribune.com

Missoulian at www.missoulian.com

Create an interview script with a famous person from Montana!

★ Research various Montanans, such as Plenty Coups, Mary Fields, Jeannette Rankin, Charles M. Russell, Phil Jackson, or Sarah Vowell.

★ Based on your research, pick one person you would most like to talk with.

★ Write a script of the interview. What questions would you ask? How would this person answer? You may want to supplement this writing project with a voice-recording dramatization of the interview.

SEE: Chapters Four, Five, Six, and Seven, pages 50, 57, 65, and 83, and the Biographical Dictionary, pages 133–136.

GO TO: http://montanakids.com/cool_stories/Famous_Montanans

ART PROJECTS

★ ★ ★

Create a PowerPoint Presentation or Visitors' Guide

Welcome to Montana!

Montana's a great place to visit and to live! From its natural beauty to its historic sites, there's plenty to see and do. In your PowerPoint presentation or brochure, highlight 10 to 15 of Montana's fascinating landmarks. Be sure to include:

★ a map of the state showing where these sites are located

★ photos, illustrations, Web links, natural history facts, geographic stats, climate and weather, plants and wildlife, and recent discoveries

SEE: Chapter Nine, pages 106–115, and Fast Facts, pages 126–127.

GO TO: The official tourism Web site for Montana at www.visitmt.com. Download and print maps, photos, and vacation ideas for tourists.

Illustrate the Lyrics to the Montana State Song
("Montana")

Use markers, paints, photos, collages, colored pencils, or computer graphics to illustrate the lyrics to "Montana." Turn your illustrations into a picture book, or scan them into PowerPoint and add music.

SEE: The lyrics to "Montana" on page 128.

GO TO: The Montana state government Web site at www.mt.gov to find out more about the origin of the state song.

State Quarter Project

From 1999 to 2008, the U.S. Mint introduced new quarters commemorating each of the 50 states in the order that they were admitted to the Union. Each state's quarter features a unique design on its back, or reverse.

GO TO: www.usmint.gov/kids and find out what's featured on the back of the Montana quarter.

★ Research the significance of the image. Who designed the quarter? Who chose the final design?

★ Design your own Montana quarter. What images would you choose for the reverse?

★ Make a poster showing the Montana quarter and label each image.

SCIENCE, TECHNOLOGY, & MATH PROJECTS

★ ★ ★

Graph Population Statistics!

★ Compare population statistics (such as ethnic background, birth, death, and literacy rates) in Montana counties or major cities.

★ In your graph or chart, look at population density and write sentences describing what the population statistics show; graph one set of population statistics and write a paragraph explaining what the graphs reveal.

SEE: Chapter Six, pages 76–79.

GO TO: The official Web site for the U.S. Census Bureau at www.census.gov and at http://quickfacts.census.gov/qfd/states/30000.html to find out more about population statistics, how they work, and what the statistics are for Montana.

Create a Weather Map of Montana!

Use your knowledge of Montana's geography to research and identify conditions that result in specific weather events. What is it about the geography of Montana that makes it vulnerable to heavy snow and to wildfires? Create a weather map or poster that shows the weather patterns over the state. Include a caption explaining the technology used to measure weather phenomena and provide data.

SEE: Chapter One, pages 15–16.

GO TO: The National Oceanic and Atmospheric Administration's National Weather Service Web site at www.weather.gov for weather maps and forecasts for Montana.

Track Endangered Species

Using your knowledge of Montana's wildlife, research which animals and plants are endangered or threatened.

★ Find out what the state is doing to protect these species.

★ Chart known populations of the animals and plants, and report on changes in certain geographic areas.

SEE: Chapter One, page 19.

GO TO: Web sites such as http://fwp.mt.gov/wildthings/tande/default.html for lists of endangered species in Montana.

Whooping crane

PRIMARY VS. SECONDARY SOURCES

★ ★ ★

What's the Diff?

Your teacher may require at least one or two primary sources and one or two secondary sources for your assignment. So, what's the difference between the two?

★ **Primary sources are original.** You are reading the actual words of someone's diary, journal, letter, autobiography, or interview. Primary sources can also be photographs, maps, prints, cartoons, news/film footage, posters, first-person newspaper articles, drawings, musical scores, and recordings. By the way, when you conduct a survey, interview someone, shoot a video, or take photographs to include in a project, you are creating primary sources!

★ **Secondary sources are what you find in encyclopedias, textbooks, articles, biographies, and almanacs.** These are written by a person or group of people who tell about something that happened to someone else. Secondary sources also recount what another person said or did. This book is an example of a secondary source.

Now that you know what primary sources are—where can you find them?

★ **Your school or local library:** Check the library catalog for collections of original writings, government documents, musical scores, and so on. Some of this material may be stored on microfilm. The Library of Congress Web site (www.loc.gov) is an excellent online resource for primary source materials.

★ **Historical societies:** These organizations keep historical documents, photographs, and other materials. Staff members can help you find what you are looking for. History museums are also great places to see primary sources firsthand.

★ **The Internet:** There are lots of sites that have primary sources you can download and use in a project or assignment.

TIMELINE

★ ★ ★

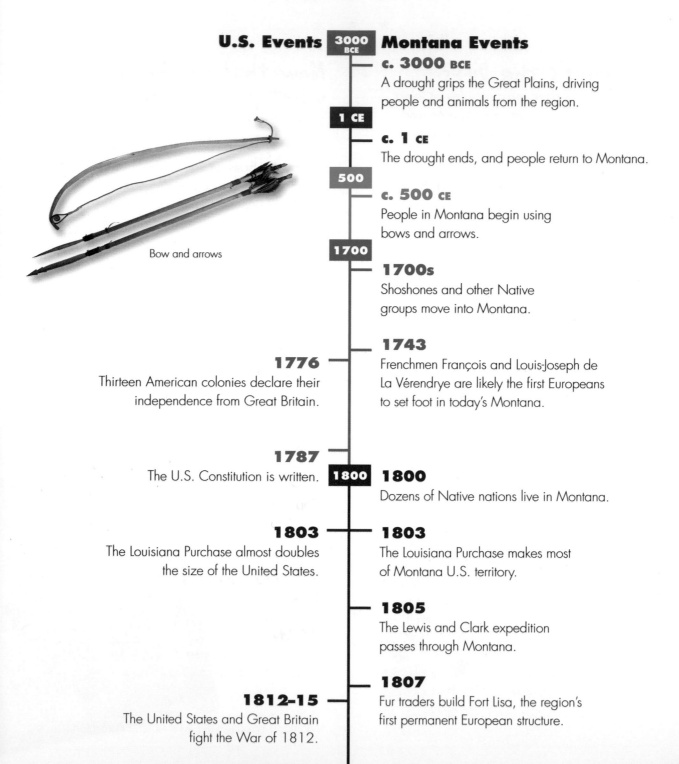

U.S. Events | 3000 BCE | **Montana Events**

c. 3000 BCE
A drought grips the Great Plains, driving people and animals from the region.

1 CE

c. 1 CE
The drought ends, and people return to Montana.

500

c. 500 CE
People in Montana begin using bows and arrows.

1700

1700s
Shoshones and other Native groups move into Montana.

1743
Frenchmen François and Louis-Joseph de La Vérendrye are likely the first Europeans to set foot in today's Montana.

1776
Thirteen American colonies declare their independence from Great Britain.

Bow and arrows

1787
The U.S. Constitution is written.

1800

1800
Dozens of Native nations live in Montana.

1803
The Louisiana Purchase almost doubles the size of the United States.

1803
The Louisiana Purchase makes most of Montana U.S. territory.

1805
The Lewis and Clark expedition passes through Montana.

1807
Fur traders build Fort Lisa, the region's first permanent European structure.

1812–15
The United States and Great Britain fight the War of 1812.

U.S. Events

1846–48
The United States fights a war with Mexico over western territories in the Mexican War.

1861–65
The American Civil War is fought between the Northern Union and the Southern Confederacy; it ends with the surrender of the Confederate army, led by General Robert E. Lee.

1866
The U.S. Congress approves the Fourteenth Amendment to the U.S. Constitution, granting citizenship to African Americans.

The Battle of the Little Bighorn

1886
Apache leader Geronimo surrenders to the U.S. Army, ending the last major Native American rebellion against the expansion of the United States into the West.

Montana Events

1841
Catholic priests establish St. Mary's Mission in the Bitterroot Mountains.

1846
The Oregon Treaty makes the Bitterroot Mountains U.S. territory.

1862
Gold is discovered at Grasshopper Creek, setting off a gold rush.

1864
The Montana Territory is established.

1870
U.S. troops massacre 173 Blackfoot people on the Marias River.

1876
Native forces defeat U.S. troops at the Battle of the Little Bighorn.

1880–90
Settlers pour into Montana, increasing the population fivefold.

1880s
Copper mining brings great wealth to Montana.

1883
The Northern Pacific Railway, running the length of Montana, is completed.

1886
Drought and freezing weather almost destroy Montana's cattle industry.

1889
Montana becomes the 41st state in the Union.

U.S. Events `1900` Montana Events

1914
Women in Montana win the right to vote.

1917–18
The United States engages in World War I.

1916
Jeannette Rankin of Missoula becomes the first woman elected to the U.S. Congress.

1920s
Drought causes many farm families to leave Montana.

1929
The stock market crashes, plunging the United States more deeply into the Great Depression.

1933
Construction begins on the Fort Peck Dam.

Building Fort Peck Dam

1941–45
The United States engages in World War II.

1951–53
The United States engages in the Korean War.

1964–73
The United States engages in the Vietnam War.

1970s
Tourism eclipses mining as the state's leading industry.

1972
Montana voters approve a new constitution.

1973
Montana passes a law requiring that land damaged by mining be returned to its natural state.

Skiing at Whitefish Mountain Resort

1991
The United States and other nations engage in the brief Persian Gulf War against Iraq.

`2000`

2000
Judy Martz is the first woman to be elected governor of Montana.

2001
Terrorists attack the United States on September 11.

2008
The United States elects its first African American president, Barack Obama.

GLOSSARY

archaeologists people who study the remains of past human societies

artifacts items created by humans, usually for a practical purpose

cavalry soldiers who ride on horseback

censured officially blamed or disapproved

corps a group working together on a special mission

discrimination unequal treatment based on race, gender, religion, or other factors

endangered in danger of becoming extinct

global warming an increase in temperatures around the globe, particularly as a result of pollution

hydroelectric power electricity generated by the force of water passing over a dam

immunity a body's ability to resist disease

infamy an evil reputation

militia an army made up of citizens trained to serve as soldiers in an emergency

mission a place created by a religious group to spread its beliefs

progressive making social improvement through government action

prospectors people who search a region for valuable minerals

rations food allowances from a given supply

segregation separation from others, according to race, class, ethnic group, religion, or other factors

threatened likely to become endangered in the foreseeable future

tributaries smaller rivers that flow into a larger river

vigilantes volunteers who try on their own to stop crime and punish criminals

white supremacist one who believes in the superiority of the white race over other races

FAST FACTS

★ ★ ★

State Symbols

State seal

Statehood date	November 8, 1889; the 41st state
Origin of state name	Spanish for "mountainous"
State capital	Helena
State nickname	Treasure State, Big Sky Country, Land of Shining Mountains
State motto	*Oro y Plata* ("Gold and Silver")
State bird	Western meadowlark
State flower	Bitterroot
State animal	Grizzly bear
State fish	Black spotted cutthroat trout
State fossil	Duck-billed dinosaur
State gemstones	Sapphire and agate
State grass	Blue bunch wheatgrass
State song	"Montana"
State tree	Ponderosa pine

Geography

Total area; rank	147,042 square miles (380,837 sq km); 4th
Land; rank	145,552 square miles (376,978 sq km); 4th
Water; rank	1,490 square miles (3,859 sq km); 26th
Inland water; rank	1,490 square miles (3,859 sq km); 15th
Geographic center	Fergus County, 11 miles (18 km) west of Lewistown
Latitude	44°26' N to 49° N
Longitude	104°2' W to 116°2' W
Highest point	Granite Peak, 12,799 feet (3,901 m), in Park County
Lowest point	Kootenai River in Lincoln County, 1,800 feet (549 m)
Largest city	Billings
Number of counties	56
Longest river	Missouri

Population

Population; rank (2007 estimate)	957,861; 44th
Density (2007 estimate)	7 persons per square mile (3 per sq km)
Population distribution (2000 census)	54% urban, 46% rural
Race (2007 estimate)	White persons: 90.7%*
	American Indian and Alaska Native persons: 6.3%*
	Asian persons: 0.7%*
	Black persons: 0.6%*
	Native Hawaiian and Other Pacific Islanders: 0.1%*
	Persons reporting two or more races: 1.7%
	Persons of Hispanic or Latino origin: 2.8%†
	White persons not Hispanic: 88.2%

* Includes persons reporting only one race.
† Hispanics may be of any race, so they are also included in applicable race categories.

Weather

Record high temperature	117°F (47°C) at Glendive on July 20, 1893, and at Medicine Lake on July 5, 1937
Record low temperature	–70°F (–57°C) at Rogers Pass on January 20, 1954
Average July temperature	68°F (20°C)
Average January temperature	20°F (–7°C)
Average yearly precipitation	11 inches (28 cm)

State flag

STATE SONG

★ ★ ★

"Montana"

Joseph E. Howard wrote the music and Charles C. Cohan wrote the words to "Montana," which was designated the state song in 1945.

Tell me of that Treasure State
Story always new,
Tell of its beauties grand
And its hearts so true.

Mountains of sunset fire
The land I love the best
Let me grasp the hand of one
From out the Golden West.

Chorus:
Montana, Montana,
Glory of the West
Of all the states from coast to coast,
You're easily the best.
Montana, Montana,
Where skies are always blue
M-O-N-T-A-N-A,
Montana, I love you.

Each country has its flow'r;
Each one plays a part,
Each bloom brings a longing hope
To some lonely heart.

Bitterroot to me is dear
Growing in my land
Sing then that glorious air
The one I understand.

(Chorus)

NATURAL AREAS AND HISTORIC SITES

★ ★ ★

National Parks

Glacier National Park preserves more than 1 million acres (400,000 ha) of forests, alpine meadows, and lakes.

Yellowstone National Park, the oldest national park in the world, attracts millions of visitors who want to see its many geysers and hot springs.

National Recreation Area

The *Bighorn Canyon National Recreation Area* features lakes, rivers, and a magnificent canyon.

National Monument

Little Bighorn Battlefield National Monument preserves the site of the 1876 battle between the U.S. Army's Seventh Cavalry and several bands of Lakota Sioux, Cheyenne, and Arapaho peoples.

National Battlefield

Big Hole National Battlefield memorializes the people who fought and died at the site during the Nez Perce War in 1877. It is part of the Nez Perce National Historical Park.

National Historical Park

Nez Perce National Historical Park, which commemorates the stories and history of the Nez Perce people, includes 38 sites in four states. The sites follow the trail the Nez Perce people took when escaping U.S. soldiers.

National Historic Site

Grant-Kohrs Ranch National Historic Site commemorates the Western cattle industry and is still a working ranch.

National Historic Trail

The *Lewis & Clark National Historic Trail* passes through Montana, following the trail of Lewis and Clark's journey.

National Forests

Montana has nine national forests: *Beaverhead-Deerlodge National Forest, Bitterroot National Forest, Custer National Forest, Flathead National Forest, Gallatin National Forest, Helena National Forest, Kootenai National Forest, Lewis and Clark National Forest,* and *Lolo National Forest.*

State Parks and Forests

Montana's state park system features 50 state park and recreation areas, including *Beaverhead Rock State Park, Parker Homestead State Park,* and *Spring Meadow Lake State Park.*

SPORTS TEAMS

★　★　★

NCAA Teams (Division I)

Montana State University *Bobcats*
University of Montana *Grizzlies*

The University of Montana women's basketball team celebrates the
Big Sky Tournament Championship in 2008.

CULTU AL INSTITUTIONS

Libraries

Montana Historical Society Research Center (Helena) contains the world's largest historical collection on the history of the Montana area.

Montana State University Library (Billings) contains significant collections on George Custer and the Battle of the Little Bighorn.

Museums

The *Museum of the Rockies* (Bozeman) features exhibits on Rocky Mountain geology, archaeology, and fossils.

The *Museum of the Plains Indians and Craft Center* (Browning) houses historical and contemporary American Indian art collections.

The *World Museum of Mining* (Butte) highlights the history of mining and the evolution of mining techniques.

The *Montana Historical Society* (Helena) houses the state's historical collections and art by Western artist Charles M. Russell.

Performing Arts

All of Montana's larger cities have community symphony orchestras and centers for the performing arts. Many cities also have community and university drama and dance groups.

Universities and Colleges

In 2006, Montana had 13 public and eight private institutions of higher learning.

ANNUAL EVENTS

January–March

National Outdoor Speedskating Championship in Butte (January)

Race to the Sky Sled Dog Race from Helena to Seeley Lake (February)

Winter Carnival in Whitefish (February)

Winter Carnival in Red Lodge (February)

April–June

Cherry Blossom Festival in Polson (May)

Governor's Cup Marathon in Helena (early June)

College National Finals Rodeo in Bozeman (June)

Music Festival in Red Lodge (June)

Montana Traditional Dixieland Jazz Festival in Helena (June)

Walleye Fishing Tournament in Havre (June)

July–September

Home of Champions Rodeo in Red Lodge (July)

Iron Ring Celebration in Poplar (July)

Libby Logger Days (July)

Livingston Roundup (July)

State Fiddlers' Contest in Polson (July)

North American Indian Days in Browning (July)

Yellowstone River Float from Livingston to Billings (July)

Wild Horse Stampede in Wolf Point (end of July)

Crow Fair in Crow Agency (August)

Festival of Nations in Red Lodge (August)

Northwest Montana Fair and Rodeo in Kalispell (August)

Sweet Pea Art Festival in Bozeman (August)

Western Montana Fair and Rodeo in Missoula (August)

Threshing Bee and Antique Show in Culbertson (September)

October–December

Pumpkin Sunday in Deer Lodge (October)

Bison Roundup near Moiese (October)

Northern International Livestock Show and Rodeo in Billings (October)

Bald Eagle Gathering near Helena (November)

Fall Camp for Cross-Country Skiers in West Yellowstone (November)

Downtown Helena Fall Art Walk (November)

Christmas Stroll in Bozeman (December)

Dorothy Baker (1907–1968) was a writer from Missoula. Her novel *Young Man with a Horn* became a popular movie starring Kirk Douglas.

Dirk Benedict (1945–) is an actor who has appeared in TV shows such as *Battlestar Galactica* and *The A-Team*. He was born in Helena and grew up in White Sulphur Springs.

Ed Bouchee (1933–) was a star baseball player in the 1950s. Born in Livingston, he played for several teams, including the Chicago Cubs.

Dana Carvey (1955–) is an actor and comedian who was born in Missoula. For many years, he did impersonations of presidents and other politicians on the TV show *Saturday Night Live*.

William A. Clark See page 62.

Sneed Collard III See page 86.

Dana Carvey

Gary Cooper (1901–1961), who was born in Helena, was a Hollywood actor. He appeared in many films from the 1920s through the 1950s, including the classic Western *High Noon* for which he won the Academy Award for Best Actor.

Margaret Craven (1901–1980) was a writer from Helena. Her works include *I Heard the Owl Call My Name*.

Marcus Daly (1841–1900) was an industrialist who was born in Ireland and became one of Montana's "copper kings." He founded the city of Anaconda.

Ivan Doig (1939–), who grew up in White Sulphur Springs, has written many novels about rural Montana. His works include *English Creek*, *Dancing at the Rascal Fair*, and *This House of Sky: Landscapes of a Western Mind*.

Mary Fields See page 57.

Ivan Doig

Alice Greenough (1902–1995) was a rodeo performer who became a member of the Cowgirl Hall of Fame. She was born in Red Lodge.

Wylie Gustafson (1961–) is a country and western singer who was born in Conrad. He is especially noted for yodeling, an art he learned from his father.

A. B. Guthrie Jr. (1901–1991), who lived in Choteau, wrote many books on the American West, including *The Way West*, which won the Pulitzer Prize for Fiction in 1950, and *The Big Sky*.

Jack Horner See page 11.

Chet Huntley (1911–1974), a TV news reporter, was born in Cardwell. He teamed with fellow reporter David Brinkley to create the *Huntley-Brinkley Report*, the most popular news show in the 1960s.

Phil Jackson

Dorothy M. Johnson

Phil Jackson (1945–), who is from Deer Lodge, played professional basketball for 13 years before becoming one of the game's leading coaches. He coached the Chicago Bulls to six championships in the 1990s and later led the Los Angeles Lakers to three championship seasons.

Dorothy M. Johnson (1905–1984), who grew up in Whitefish, wrote books about the American West such as *Buffalo Woman* and *Beulah Bunny Tells All*. Three of her stories were made into movies.

Evel Knievel (1938–2007) was a motorcycle daredevil who was born in Butte. His televised motorcycle stunts included soaring his motorcycle over 16 cars parked side by side. He broke 40 bones over the course of his career.

Ella Knowles See page 92.

Jeff Kober (1953–) is a movie and TV actor from Billings. He has appeared on popular shows such as *Buffy the Vampire Slayer* and *NYPD Blue*.

Jerry Kramer (1936–), who was born in Jordan, was an NFL football player. His greatest years came as a lineman with the Green Bay Packers.

Myrna Loy (1905–1993), a movie star during the 1930s and 1940s, was born in Radersburg. Her popular films include *The Thin Man*.

David Lynch (1946–) is a screenwriter and director born in Missoula. His works include the acclaimed film *The Elephant Man* and the TV series *Twin Peaks*.

Mike Mansfield See page 93.

Dave McNally (1942–2002) was an all-star baseball player from Billings. He played most of his career with the Baltimore Orioles, helping the team win two World Series.

George Montgomery (1916–2000) was an actor born in Brady. After growing up on Montana ranches, he took his skill in horse riding to Hollywood, where he acted in Western movies. He was also a self-taught sculptor and created busts of fellow actors such as John Wayne and Ronald Reagan.

Adam Morrison

Adam Morrison (1984–) is a basketball player who overcame childhood diabetes to become a college star at Gonzaga. He now plays for the Charlotte Bobcats of the National Basketball Association. He was born in Glendive.

Dan Mortensen (1968–) is a champion rodeo performer who was born in Billings to a family of Montana cowboys. He appeared in his first rodeo at the age of 10 and by age 12 was riding bulls at rodeos.

Brent Musburger (1939–) is a TV sportscaster who grew up in Billings. He began his professional career by writing sports articles for Chicago newspapers.

Christopher Paolini (1983–) is a writer who published his first fantasy novel, the wildly popular *Eragon*, when he was just a teenager. He grew up in Paradise Valley.

Plenty Coups See page 50.

Plenty Coups

Charley Pride

Charley Pride (1938–) is a country music singer who once lived in Helena and Great Falls. He is one of a few African Americans to achieve fame as a country and western singer. His biggest hit, released in 1971, was "Kiss an Angel Good Morning."

Jeannette Rankin See page 65.

Charles M. Russell See page 83.

Sacagawea See page 35.

Lois Fister Steele (1939–) works to increase the number of Native American doctors in the United States. She grew up on the Fort Peck Reservation in Poplar.

Joseph Kemp Toole See page 60.

Sarah Vowell (1969–) is a writer, humorist, and radio commentator. Her books include *The Partly Cloudy Patriot* and *Assassination Vacation*. She grew up in Bozeman.

Dennis Washington (1934–) is a business leader from Missoula. He began his career in the construction industry and soon became a mine owner. He is also involved in real estate, shipping, and railroads. In 2007, he was number 102 on a list of the richest people in the United States.

Michelle Williams (1980–) is an actor who was born in Kalispell. She broke into acting as a teen star on the TV series *Dawson's Creek*. She has also appeared in the films *The Station Agent* and *I'm Not There*.

Michelle Williams

Robert Yellowtail (1889–1988) was a Crow leader who helped enlarge the Crow Reservation and encouraged education among the Crow people. He was from Lodge Grass.

York See page 36.

Sarah Vowell

RESESOURCES

★ ★ ★

BOOKS

Nonfiction

Dougherty, Michael, and Heidi Pfeil Dougherty. *The Ultimate Montana Atlas and Travel Encyclopedia*. Bozeman, Mont.: Ultimate Press, 2005.

Marsh, Carole. *Montana Native Americans*. Peachtree City, Ga.: Gallopade International, 2004.

Marx, Trish. *Jeannette Rankin: First Lady of Congress*. New York: Margaret K. McElderry Books, 2006.

Merrill, Andrea, and Judy Jacobson. *Montana Almanac*. Helena, Mont.: TwoDot Publishing, 1997.

Shirley, Gayle C. *Amazing Animals of Montana: Incredible True Stories*. Guilford, Conn.: Globe Pequot, 2005.

Spencer, Janet. *Montana Trivia*. Helena, Mont.: Riverbend Publishing, 2005.

Walker, Paul. *Remember Little Bighorn: Indians, Soldiers, and Scouts Tell Their Stories*. Washington, D.C.: National Geographic Press, 2006.

Williams, Judith. *The Discovery and Mystery of a Dinosaur Named Jane*. Berkeley Heights, N.J.: Enslow Publishers, 2007.

Fiction

Corcoran, Barbara. *Wolf at the Door*. New York: Atheneum, 1993.

Larson, Kirby. *Hattie Big Sky*. New York: Delacorte, 2006.

Thomas, Jane Resh. *Blind Mountain*. New York: Clarion Books, 2006.

Walter, Dave. *Montana Campfire Tales*. Helena, Mont.: TwoDot Publishing, 1997.

DVDs

Discoveries . . . America: Montana. Bennet-Watt Media, 2007.
Flathead Valley, Montana, and Glacier National Park. Travelscope LLC, 2008.
Glacier National Park. Questar, 2003.
Libby, Montana. High Plains Films, 2005.
A River Runs Through It. Columbia Tristar Home Video, 1999.
Weekend Explorer: Whitefish, Montana. Barnstormer Productions, 2005.

WEB SITES AND ORGANIZATIONS

Montana History
www.metnet.mt.gov/teachmthistory/index.html
To find out more about Montana's past and present.

Montana Kids
www.montanakids.com
Learn about Big Sky Country at this fun, interactive Web site.

Montana: Official State Travel Information Site
http://visitmt.com
Find out more about Montana history, wildlife, and the many things you can do in the state.

Montana's Official State Web Site
www.mt.gov
For more information about Montana's state government.

Official State Travel Information Site: Montana's Indian Nations
http://indiannations.visitmt.com
For detailed information about the state's Native Americans.

INDEX

★ ★ ★

AUTHOR'S TIPS AND SOURCE NOTES

★　★　★

I read many books while researching this project. Among the most useful were *Montana: An Uncommon Land* by K. Ross Toole and *Montana: A History of Two Centuries* by Michael P. Malone, Richard B. Roeder, and William L. Lang. I also had fun reading a book called *Montana Trivia* by Janet Spencer. The Internet was extremely useful in writing this book. It is a great tool for research, but it is important to make sure that the Web sites you are using are authoritative. Sites sponsored by the government, libraries, or universities can usually be trusted.